Listening
for God

A Minister's Journey

Through Silence and Doubt

Renita J. Weems

Simon & Schuster

SIMON & SCHUSTER
Rockefeller Center
1230 Avenue of the Americas
New York, NY 10020

SIMON & SCHUSTER and colophon are registered
trademarks of Simon & Schuster Inc.

Designed by Karolina Harris
Manufactured in the United States of America

1   3   5   7   9   10   8   6   4   2

Library of Congress Cataloging-in-Publication Data
Weems, Renita J.
Listening for God : a minister's journey through
silence and doubt / Renita J. Weems.
p.   cm.
Includes bibliographical references.
1. Weems, Renita J.   2. Afro-American Methodists—Biography
3. Methodists—United States—Biography.   4. Afro-American
women clergy—Biography.   5. Methodist Church—
United States—Clergy—Biography.   I. Title.
BX8473.W44A3   1999
287'.8'092—dc21
[B]   98-54817
                                                                  CIP

ISBN 0-684-83323-9

To
Martin L. Espinosa, who freed me to hear God,
and
Savannah Nia Weems Espinosa,
who saw to it that I stayed present to the Presence

Contents

Contents

CHAPTER THREE:

THE MYSTERY OF MARRIAGE AND MOTHERING

CHAPTER FOUR:

THE MYSTERY OF MIRACLES

.

I have often been told that when one first turns to God, one is greeted with brilliant Yes answers to prayers. For a long time that was true for me. But then, when he has you hooked, he starts to say No. This has been, indeed, my experience. But it has been more than a No answer lately; after all, No is an answer. It is the silence, the withdrawal, which is so devastating. The world is difficult enough with God; without him it is a hideous joke.

MADELEINE L'ENGLE, *The Irrational Season*

Listening
for God

Preface

Some years ago when, as a minister, I was feeling that God had withdrawn from me and I was going through what I can only describe now as a spiritual breakdown—questioning seriously my belief in God, prayer, religious texts, and rituals to such a degree that I couldn't bear to talk or read about anything having to do with the sacred—it never dawned upon me to retire my clergy stole and leave the ministry. Even though I couldn't recall the last time I'd felt anything faintly resembling religious awe or spiritual ecstasy, I never stopped praying. I could have walked away from the ordained ministry, of course, and retreated to the lofty heights of academia, where I was teaching Old Testament studies (and still do); and I could have stopped writing and conducting seminars and workshops about spiritual formation and mystical encounters, topics I felt I no longer had the faintest experience with. But I decided against that. I chose to remain a minister and to remain actively involved in a local congregation, leading worship, administering the sacraments, and leading prayers. It dawned on me that ministry was precisely where I needed to be *because* I no longer recognized the presence of God in my life. I continued to be a minister—*and* I railed against God. Every Sunday I donned my clergy stole, prayed for the sick, blessed the sacraments and distributed them to outstretched palms, spoke movingly (I'm told) about faith, and then came home to sit and stare at the darkness in my study. Likewise I continued to talk and write about fulfilling moments in the inner journey, all the while staggering about in my own inner abyss.

Two things kept me afloat during that period in my life. One was my own honesty. I tried at first to lie about what was going on inside my heart, acting as though everything was fine, pretending as a minister and writer that I had an active prayer life and enjoyed intimacy with God. That lie went on for far longer than it should have. I'm grateful that I had a few close friends in my life, themselves ministers, who knew me well enough to know that something was wrong and, when I disclosed to them my secret, loved me enough not to denounce me. Eventually I gave up pretending, however, and confessed to God—loudly, bitterly, sometimes in blasphemous tones—that it felt as though I had been seduced out into waters where God knew I couldn't swim, and had been left abandoned, without a life jacket, to flail about and figure out for myself how not to drown. After what felt like years of flailing about, when I saw that (for reasons I still haven't been able to fathom) I wasn't going to drown, I began to calm down and stop fighting the waters. I continued to protest to God that things weren't the same between us, but by now my complaints were less bellicose. I accepted the silence as a new way of communicating with the divine and learned to perceive God in my life in new, amusing, laughable, glorious ways. I am convinced that my honesty is what kept me available to the miracles of grace that began popping up all around me.

The second thing that kept me from walking away from God was the honesty of others who'd survived similar periods in their spiritual journey. Had it not been for the stories of other women and men who have endured seasons of silence between God and themselves, I would have felt hopelessly alone. Many classic and contemporary writings reached canonical status in my heart, despite my Protestant upbringing, because they nourished me in the lowest moments of my journey. Some of the writers were Catholic, others were Jewish, several were Protestant. Many of them, I am happy to say, were women mystics and poets writing about the lonelier zones of the spiritual path. Many others were male writers—mystics, poets, and clergymen alike—who have written eloquently and authoritatively about such important things as God, eternity, mortality, suffering, and hope. By feasting on the writings of classic and contemporary writers, I was reminded that while it is true that every spiritual journey is different, some paths nevertheless are well worn and are worth following.

Listening for God focuses on the lessons I have learned in this journey of feeling lost and disoriented. I offer the intimate conversations of *Listening for God,* filled as it is with secret protestations, private doubts, and grateful glimpses of the divine, as proof that even seasoned explorers of the soul can get lost and disconsolate along the way. But no matter how lonely, quiet, and unpredictable the journey, with patient listening holy silence can become music. Retracing my painful steps along this journey helps to remind us all of the ups and downs of intimacy with God and to encourage us along the way each time we feel we should be further along in the journey and have been thinking about turning back. *Listening for God* follows me through the ups and downs of a believer's journey, through the mysteries, also, of my journey as a girl growing up in the Pentecostal South, my ordination into ministry, and the many revelations from God that come with being a wife and mother. Through these prayers, poems, journal entries, and conversations I had with God, myself, and others, I had to invent new ways to touch, feel, smell, taste, and find my way to God. Sometimes I succeeded. Sometimes I failed. But what I learned about perseverance and faithfulness in staying on course is offered here through the prism of my chaotic life.

Frustrated to discover that a journey I thought would be a linear tug in one direction has amounted to a journey of lurches and stops, I have been reluctant at times to admit out loud that mine was a journey of growth spurts followed by what felt like long periods of hushed decay. For years I thought something was wrong with me. I didn't know how to talk about the jerks and lulls, the tugs and pulls, the endless crawling, when one seemingly never moves on but is forever beginning anew, always returning to the same spot, albeit stronger and wiser. How do you talk about an inner journey that doesn't progress along a straight line but is, instead, circular and leads one back to the same beginning spot time and time again? How do you describe a journey that leaves you feeling sometimes as though you're not getting anywhere, that you're no better off than you were when you first started? How do you follow someone you can't always recognize? Perhaps we're all fooling ourselves and are only spinning straw into words by pretending to be able to describe the inner journey. Perhaps the wisest thing to do is to take God's cue and be silent.

Although a deluge of books has been written about various aspects of the inner journey, much of what has been written in recent years appears to be directed to the novitiate, the recent traveler, the newcomer to the inward journey. Many of these books focus on the intoxicating joys of the inward journey, but not enough has been written about the long dry seasons.

What about those of us who are beyond the first blush of the spiritual journey, who after a period of dramatic awakening now feel as if we have hit a brick wall and our prayers have been met with silence? It is comforting to know that even in the book that passes itself off as the word of God, there are testimonies of people who railed at God for what sometimes felt like God's cruel refusal to speak. Biblical poets and psalmists alike longed for intimacy with God and complained about God's seeming detachment and heartless silence. I read a text like Psalm 42 and I know I have met a kindred soul who knew what it felt like to be abandoned by God.

> As a deer yearns
> for flowing streams,
> so I yearn
> for you, my God.
> I thirst for God,
> the living God;
> where can I go to see
> the face of God?
> I have no food but tears,
> day and night,
> as all day long I am taunted,
> "Where is your God?"

I have been nurtured all my life by religious texts like this one. In fact, my love for this and other texts like it is what lured me years ago into my vocational paths as minister, Bible professor, and writer. Even eight years of rigorous academic study of the biblical literature have not been able to curb my affection for these intrepid psalms. They have been my chief source of comfort when sometimes, as a woman and as an African

American, I have been left to believe from the teachings of the church that I have no rights to God. If these psalms and similar writings were absent from the Bible, my spirit might have withered away long ago.

Listening for God will offer for many a first-time glimpse into the private yearnings of a minister who is also a wife and a mother, who, unlike many of the poets, celibates, and mystics who have written on various aspects of spiritual formation, does not have the luxury of going off into a study to write for sustained periods of uninterrupted solitude and cannot get away to the mountains or to a monastery for quiet time with God. If God was going to speak to me, God would just have to do it amidst the clutter of family, the noise of pots and pans, the din of a hungry toddler screaming from the backseat during rush hour traffic, and the hassles of the workplace. It's hard to find the time and energy to pray when you're averaging four to six hours of sleep a day. If God was silent because God was upset about how little time I had to sit still, then God would just have to increase the number of hours in a day, I reasoned. Women have for centuries been made to feel guilty because in our ongoing struggle to balance solitude and intimacy, we've found ourselves, often for reasons not always of our doing, having to give up the former for the sake of the latter. While I agree completely with those who argue that solitude and quiet are necessary conditions for replenishing the soul and the psyche, and that prayer thrives on stillness before God, the greatest challenge for me as a minister and a mother was to stop always blaming myself and feeling guilty. The lesson was learning how to hear God in different ways and in different places—which in my case meant in the noisiness of my life and in the seasons of divine silence, when God seemed withdrawn and distant. While one thinks of clerics as those who routinely scurry off to lofty spiritual planes to commune with God, the truth is that the soul can bear only so much of the lofty. In fact, some of the most memorable encounters with grace are those that erupt into the daily details of mundane, ordinary life. The challenge for me was to cease looking for God in the spectacular and to take delight in the joys and rewards of everyday fidelities.

I am finally ready to talk about that difficult period in my life publicly and am willing to share with others what I learned—not because my love affair with God and mystery has returned. It has not—not really, not like before. I can share the experience now because I am no longer afraid of God's silence. Nor am I ashamed of having doubted myself and God. By peering in on my struggles with highs and lows in the inner journey, my struggle to balance solitude and intimacy, my learning the lessons of the different seasons of the journey, readers will hopefully learn something of value for their own journey. By sharing conversations I've had with God and myself through more than twenty years of journaling, I hope readers will come to accept the variety of forms that prayer can take.

Finally, I admit that most of the spiritual pain I have experienced over the years has been the result of my failure to surrender to the season in which I found myself. Rather than facing the silent seasons straight on and allowing myself to experiment with new ways of encountering the divine, I have wasted many seasons by castigating myself for what felt like a deep freeze within. I have blamed myself and those around me for my constant fatigue and my inability to pray. Worst yet, I have spent the greater part of the season pretending to feel something I didn't feel. I have preached when (sometimes) I should have been, if not silent, then less eloquent. I have spoken falsely (and unpersuasively, I know now) about inspiration when I should have admitted that there was none. I didn't know how to trust the silent journey to do its work. I didn't know that just because I'd lost my enthusiasm for the spiritual journey didn't mean that I'd lost my way on the spiritual journey. I had to fall in and out of love with God a thousand times before I finally figured out that it was all right to fall in and out of love a thousand times, that just because God is silent doesn't mean that God is absent. I had grown so accustomed to believing in a God who spoke thunderously and in spectacular ways that I didn't think I could survive when it came time to stumble in divine silence. Just as noise cannot always be helped, neither is God's silence always our fault. It is just part of the journey. I had to learn how to pay attention. I had to learn how to perceive the divine in new ways and in new places. I had to stop peeping behind altars for epiphanies and learn to let the lull between epiphanies teach me new ways for communicating with God, for reverencing the holy, and for listening for God.

Chapter One

The Mystery of Silence and Prayer

Stumbling in the Silence

If you can't pray—at least say your prayers.

GEORGES BERNANOS

No one is ever prepared to endure the long silence that
follows intimacy. No one is prepared to face it when it comes
after lovemaking. No one is prepared to face it when it follows
a season of intimacy with God. It is the hardest thing to talk
about, and it is the hardest thing in the spiritual journey to
prepare for. The long silence between intimacies, the inter-
minable pause between words, the immeasurable seconds between pulses, the quiet between epiphanies, the hush after
ecstasy, the listening for God—this is the spiritual journey,
learning how to live in the meantime, between the last time
you heard from God and the next time you hear from God.

Just as there are seasons of the year, there are seasons of the
soul, changes in the atmospheric pressure that sweep over the
human spirit. We move in and out of them, often without
being aware of them, almost unconsciously, and frequently
without appreciation for the new experiences they bring our
way. Where does one begin talking about the dips and curves
along the spiritual journey? How does a minister admit that
she's been left slumping toward mystery more than she has
been grasping mystery? What lessons have pulled me
through? What happened to all those prayers I prayed and
the ones I gave up praying along the way? It seems always that
the task before me was learning how to distinguish when it

was God who seemed hidden and when it was I who was hiding, and above all, learning how to wait out the time until we found our way back to each other.

Ministers rarely talk about the long dry periods in their spiritual journey. I know they don't because I am one, and I have rarely been willing to bring up the matter in public for fear that listeners would view me as a spiritual fraud. How does one who is supposedly an expert on prayer and spiritual disciplines admit that there are times when her own heart is unable to get through to the God she recommends to others? How does a minister admit that she hasn't heard from God in a long, long time? It is much easier and safer to talk about the springtime of faith, when the desire for inward journeying is insatiable and belief in mystery is irrepressible.

To admit that in the spiritual journey, highs are brief, sporadic, and rare and that the human heart experiences far longer periods of dullness, emptiness, and silence can be threatening. If people accept that inspiration and ecstasy are fleeting, hard-to-come-by experiences, then what is there to look forward to, if all we can expect is to stumble in the dark? To admit that it's all a stumble seems like an admission of failure—and Protestant ministers have a particularly difficult time admitting their defeats. Blame it on our dissident origins and our works-righteousness inheritance, which resulted in years of being told that if our prayers were met with silence, then the fault lay with no one but ourselves. Or blame it on the hardy dosage of homilies we've endured (and have ourselves given) that have insisted upon viewing God as readily available, waiting only to be sought after, invited in, and embraced. When this is your spiritual legacy, it's difficult to admit aloud to feeling adrift. It's even more difficult to admit to the times when praying feels like a hollow ritual and the closest you can bring yourself to praying is to read about prayer.

The truth is that this journey is best characterized as periods of ecstasy and periods of melancholy; seasons when I can feel the presence of the sacred in my life and seasons when the perception and even the memory of the sacred have all but evaporated from the soul; moments of deep, abiding faith and moments of quiet despair; times of calm and times of clutter; moments when prayer is music and moments when I cannot abide the sound of prayer. Stumbling, staggering, slouching, and crawling forward is not the whole story, to be sure. But stumbling, staggering, slouching, and crawling feel as though they've been the largest part of my journey. It's not possible to tell everything that has happened along the way. I've probably forgotten more than I remember. Nevertheless, fleeting glimpses of the holy that have surfaced from time to time— however faintly, briefly, and above all mysteriously—will always be regarded as miracles of grace to me.

An ancient Jewish legend first came across my desk years ago while I was studying for my comprehensive exams as a graduate student, reminding me of the healing power of stories. The next time I encountered the legend was years later while reading Clarissa Pinkola Estes's tiny little book *The Gift of Story*. No longer a graduate student, I was by this time a professor reeling under the pressure of trying to balance a career as a scholar and the demands of family and love. Both times the legend found me when I was beginning to feel as though bits and pieces of crucial knowledge were slipping away from me as I sat up at night grasping for information that my superiors approved of. Sometimes information gets in the way of knowledge, I eventually concluded. Even now this ancient Jewish legend reminds me how important stories are in helping one find one's way through darkness. On those many occasions when I have not been able either to feel or sense God's divine presence and have grown exasperated by the effort of it all, it is enough simply to cling to the memory of a memory with God. Sometimes just the memory of once having sensed God's nearness, no matter how faintly, no matter how long ago, has been enough to keep me on this journey, convincing me not to turn back, leaving me cherishing the knowledge known intuitively by my soul, even though I no longer remember how my soul first came to know it.

The story is one of the legends of the Baal Shem Tov ("master of God's name") told by his followers, the Hasidim, a Jewish sect of Eastern Europe, which he founded around the middle of the eighteenth century and which lives on to this day. Hasidic teaching centers on rebirth, believing that renewal is possible.

Perceiving that he was dying, the Baal Shem Tov called for his disciples and said, "I have acted as intermediary for you, and now when I am gone you must do this for yourselves. You know the place in the forest where I call to God? Stand there in the place and do the same. Light a fire as you have been instructed to do, and say the prayer as you learned. Do all these and God will come."

Shortly afterward, the Baal Shem Tov died. The first generation of followers did exactly as he had said, and sure enough, God came as always. After this generation passed, the second generation had forgotten how to light the fire the way the Baal Shem Tov had instructed. Nevertheless, they faithfully made the pilgrimage to the special place in the forest and said the prayer they had been instructed to pray. And sure enough, God showed up.

A third generation came along, who had forgotten how to

light the fire and no longer remembered the place in the forest where they should stand. But they said the prayer as the Baal Shem Tov had instructed. And again God showed up.

By the fourth generation, no one was around who remembered how to light the fire or where the special place was in the forest. Neither was anyone alive who could recall the prayer the Baal Shem Tov had instructed his followers to pray. But there was one person who remembered the story about the fire, the forest, and the prayer and delighted in telling it over and over. And sure enough, God came.

Often when I lose my way I rely on stories to get me through the deafening silence. I stand in the pulpit before a waiting congregation, open the folder where I've tucked my sermon, and nothing comes to my mind. No grand truths. No proclamations. No eloquent speeches. I'm fresh out of oracles. Nothing but stories. I set out to preach on the doctrine of grace, and nothing comes to mind but stories of grace.

A certain woman with ten coins, precious to no one but herself, loses one, and after a few moments of panic and fright, she lights a lamp, sweeps the entire house, and searches diligently for the coin she had lost. Upon finding it, she calls together all her friends, who are baffled by all the ruckus she has created over a simple coin. But she knows the true value of one coin when you're down to your last ten. She knows how easy it is to lose and how rare it is to find precious items. She knows that there's more to celebrate than meets the eye. In order to find her coin, she had to sort and sweep through the clutter in her home. And that itself was as much a cause for celebration as finding the precious coin. To find what you're looking for right smack in the midst of life's clutter is a miracle of grace. It is the story of losing something you couldn't bear to lose and finding more than what you lost.

I have lost my faith a thousand times, only to find it nine-hundred-and-ninety-nine times. Belief in mystery has waned and reappeared repeatedly throughout the journey. I wonder whether God is as weary of me as I am sometimes of my own soul. This on-again, off-again love affair with the sacred is unnerving. But it is, oddly enough, also fascinating. As frightening as it is to lose one's way on a journey one started out on confident of the route ahead, there is also something challenging about starting over, however ludicrous that may sound, of having the chance to experience the divine once more as though it were the first time.

Around and Around

Autumn to winter, winter into spring,
Spring into summer, summer into—
So rolls the changing year, and so we change;
Motion so swift, we know not that we move.

DINAH MARIA MULOCK CRAIK

Outside my front window are three crape myrtle trees I planted a few years back when we moved into our home. I love the way they explode into a deep pink bloom just when everything else in my garden is beginning to wilt and brown from the summer heat. Every year that they bloom I find reasons to move the furniture around in the house so I can get a better view out the front window. I use their bloom as my reminder that the summer is almost over and that a new school year is right around the bend and I'd better pack as much fun as possible in these last remaining weeks of summer. But the problem is that my crape myrtle trees never bloom the same time every year. The first year they bloomed in the second week of August. The second year they bloomed in the last week of July. This year I thought I noticed the first bud during the middle of July, when it was so hot everything outside looked as though it was melting from the heat. So soon? I asked myself as I walked back and forth in front of the window, trying to get a better view. I get to enjoy their luscious color for only four to six weeks before they shed their leaves, and then I have to wait another year before their color returns. In the meantime, I change my whole life around to accommodate them. And it's worth it. I can't say exactly when they will return to me next year, but I know I'll be here waiting with my chair in the window for the first sign that the mood around these parts is changing.

Seasons are not stages I learn from the view outside my window. They are neither linear nor chartable. They do not begin and end at predictable times, and no two seasons are alike. Seasons are cyclical. We move in and out of them a thousand times as our spirits grow and stretch. We know that a new one is upon us by noticing the changes in the texture of what is going on inside us. The inner atmosphere has changed. Perhaps a hush comes over the soul. Praying hurts. It's harder to focus. After a period of devouring everything written about the awakening of the spirit, we let weeks go by without visiting the altar deep inside us. After a period of seizing every opportunity possible to steal away to quiet and meditation, we experience months in which noise is the chant of saints.

As painful as they may be to endure, seasons are a welcome change. Deep within us is an internal clock regulating when it is time to gaze and when it is time to glimpse, when it is time to speak and when it is time to listen. We will gaze again, but for now we must content ourselves with a glimpse. We will speak again, but in the meanwhile we must be satisfied with listening.

Moving in and out of the seasons of the soul means above all to grow in fits and jerks, lurches and stops, leaps and crawls, and *for the most part.* This becomes clear when the spiritual journey is placed within the context of ordinary life, where the seasons of the soul intersect with the chaos of a full life (in my case, marriage, motherhood, ministry, scholarship, writing, living). We hope we are better human beings for becoming mindful and attentive to the spiritual side. If we are not, we will settle for being better listeners *for the most part.* We're never as far along as we think, because the spiritual journey is circular. We are always repeating ourselves, returning to old themes, reexamining the same issue from a different angle and from the vantage point of a different season. We don't move on; we return wiser.

Even ministers on the journey lose their way. Even specialists in prayer at some point lose interest in prayer. We struggle. We have doubts. We grow afraid. We become bored. We are tempted to walk away. Sometimes we do. But some of us return, and walk away, and return again and again. Why? Because the point of a journey is the going, the movement, the traveling, not just the arriving.

Surrender to the Silence

Waiting sometimes is the only thing left to do. You learn to wait, or you forfeit the lesson you were supposed to learn.

ANONYMOUS

Call it *prayer block,* a *spiritual lull,* the *wilderness experience,* the *dark night of the soul.* But eventually and invariably we all find ourselves suddenly wrenched into an inner abyss. For a while I blamed my prayer block on the energy spent trying to find bliss in a marriage that, given our feverish schedules, seemed always in need of reinventing. I blamed it on feeling constantly fatigued by all that went into rearing a headstrong but delightfully bewitching toddler whose needs frequently outstripped my own. I blamed it on the absurd juggling act of teaching, writing, speaking, and traveling that frequently left me a mere sentence away from babbling in public. (How many times have I awakened in the middle of the night in my bed at home or in a strange hotel room and asked myself, What city am I in? and, Is the speech over?) Eventually I had to admit that for as far back as I could remember—which in my case was from the days when I was a teenager eking out a faith in a small storefront Pentecostal church in Atlanta—I have anguished over what has appeared to me as the on-again, off-again character of my spiritual journey. The occasional periods of inspiration and awe seem always to be followed by longer periods of spiritual ennui. In a tradition that took religious ecstasy as proof of spiritual legitimacy, I often felt like a fraud back then for pretending to feel something I rarely felt. I thought something was wrong with me. I recall now the long prayers, the quiet tears, the secret longings, the fasts for days on end in hopes that God would fill me with awe and ecstasy. For years I felt like a failure. For several decades more, after carving out work for myself as a minister and biblical scholar, I continued to be dogged by guilt and shame.

One day I decided to surrender. After months, perhaps years, of pretending to feel something I didn't feel, I decided to confess to the deep freeze that for a long time had had me in its grip. I stopped scolding my heart because of my inability to pray as I once had. I stopped harassing my soul about my failure to feel God's presence when I prayed or listened to sacred music or stood in the pulpit to speak. And I stopped badgering God for a sign, a gesture, a sound, some indication that I hadn't lost my way, that I needn't walk away from years of ministry, preaching, counseling, teaching in a seminary, and writing what some term "inspirational" books. Slowly, gradually, I began accepting the possibility that something inside me had changed. My soul no longer responded to the same spiritual stimuli. When finally I stopped flogging myself for the hollow feeling I'd been carrying around inside for months, I began to notice a pattern. After every high there came a spiritual low. After months of maturing in my prayer life and of feeling myself becoming increasingly sensitive to the nearness and presence of the divine in my surroundings, I noticed myself becoming spiritually listless and unable to muster any passion for the disciplines I'd undertaken to nurture the inward journey. It was as if I had slammed into a brick wall, spiritually speaking. Indeed, for as long as I could remember giving myself willingly, gladly over to a belief in mystery, I remembered experiencing periods when I was barely able to stand to hear my own prayers. And thinking back on it, I realized that this wasn't the first time something in me had shut down. The soul flourishes and withers scores of times in the face of the sublime.

Rummaging lately through some old journals, I came across a poem that I wrote almost twenty years ago. I read it and was stunned to discover how much things both change and stay the same. Even back then, I knew my relationship with God was changing. And twenty years later, I am amazed to see how little I have changed.

15 June 1980

I usedta bow,
now I stand
before God's throne.

I usedta close my eyes,
now I stare
straight ahead.

I usedta do what was expected,
now I do what I must
to make this faith
faithful to me.

I usedta be afraid of God,
now I take my chances
and wait
and wait
tapping my feet,
listening for God.

Even back in my twenties I was trying to find new ways to pray. I was trying to learn how to pray over the noise of a full life. I decided to take my chances with the silence, complaining that if the deep freeze was my fault, then if God was trying to get my attention, God would just have to learn to yell over the sounds of a life being lived. In the end, God didn't have to yell. I learned to trust the silence after years of fighting against it. I learned to let go of my naive belief that breaking out into goose bumps at talk of the sacred was a signal of intimacy with God. I learned to trust the winter months of faith, when it's difficult to remember why one ever bothered to believe. I stopped being so hard on myself and demanding that, as a wife, scholar, and writer, I should always feel excited about what I was doing, or that I should, as a mother and a minister, always sparkle with alertness and insight. This was hard to accept in a culture where, at the first sign of dullness or tedium or monotony, it's all right to give up, walk away, or try something new in hopes of finding new meaning, new thrills, new satisfaction. I stopped complaining about "going through the motions." I decided it was all right to pray (whether in new or old ways) and not feel anything. The point was to pray, whatever way I could bear at the moment. Rituals are routines that force us to live faithfully even when we no longer feel like being faithful. Until our heart has the time to arouse itself and find its way back to those we love, rituals make us show up for duty.

Neither my years in seminary nor those devoted to doctorate work in biblical studies prepared me for these periodic pulls into darkness, when prayer hurt and when journeying inward felt like a walk through a burning corridor. While loss, grief, illness, and disappointment certainly have a way of hurling us into a spiritual abyss, not all declines can be traced to a specific cause, nor can they always be easily predicted or charted. Eventually we have to accept that dying and rising, freezing and thawing, resting and rebounding, sleeping and awakening are the necessary conditions for all growth and creativity. The journey of the soul unfolds in a continual cycle, much like the seasons of nature. Spring brings a renewal of growth and energy, summer is a time of strength and confidence, and in the fall we are ablaze with insight. And then comes winter, the season of myriad agonies. As one preacher from ancient times put it so well, "For everything there is a season, and a time for everything under heaven." One of the most painful lessons is learning how to appreciate the hush of winter, when more growth takes place underground than above ground, and there in quiet, unnoticeable ways.

Eventually I had to learn that sometimes less is more. I learned to recognize the seasons of my journey. I learned to listen to my soul and to give it the much needed rest it clamored for. I gave myself permission to stop thinking I had to be superb all the time; it was all right to stutter and putter along. I discovered that it was all right no longer to remember what in former seasons I thought was so wonderful about ministry, marriage, mothering, and the spiritual process. It would come back to me.

Winter returns a thousand times. But so does spring. Even though it's easy to become overwhelmed by the gloominess, and although an occasional wallow in self-pity makes eminent sense (to me, anyway), there are things to be gained from staying put, taking it a day at a time, slowing down, and giving love, hope, and renewal a chance. It's possible to live through winter. And when we do, we're glad, for there are lessons learned in the winter that not only cannot be learned in the spring but must be mastered in order to appreciate the spring.

Believing in Believing

Lord, I believe. Help my unbelief.

It never occurred to me, because no one ever told me, that I would one day as a minister stop believing—stop believing in God as I once had, stop believing in the religion I had been practicing most of my life, stop believing in what I was doing, stop believing that my life as minister, professor of Bible, and writer made any sense. Had I been warned that this day was coming, I might have been more careful. I would have watched for the telltale signs. I might have thought to protect myself against the wear and tear on a life of faith. I could have taken care to tend more assiduously to the nicks and scrapes a praying heart endures over the years—the unanswered prayers, the weeks of not being able to pray, the contradictions, the hypocrisy in the church, the months of living with the silence of God.

But I didn't know. I didn't notice that bits and pieces of my faith were eroding away. One day I just looked around and the passion for prayer was gone.

It is enough for me these days just to believe in believing.

Why didn't I listen to those around me (professors, colleagues, ministers) when they said that I couldn't keep this up much longer, this trying to juggle faith with the cold, hard gaze of objectivity? Praying for the sick, administering the sacraments, mounting pulpits with sermon notes, counseling the distressed, churning out pastoral remarks for the church newsletter—these tasks call for a certitude that my scholarly self has been trained to mock. "How can you hope to be taken seriously as a scholar if you insist upon taking part in all that mumbo jumbo in the church?" asked colleagues with raised eyebrows when word circulated that I was actively involved in church work. "How can you be a scholar when you talk so passionately and intimately about God?" colleagues in ministry and lay members in church often sidled up to me and inquired. I had no answer for either group. I didn't understand it myself. How do you explain belief and unbelief being able to occupy the same space? You can't. But I was confident that the two could coexist amicably in me. Each in its own way reinforced the other, I told myself. Nature, it seemed to me, had dealt me a cruel hand, making me something of a spiritual hunchback, twisting and misshaping my inner self in ways that left me at heart *both* a cynic *and* a believer. I had witnessed and experienced enough evil in the world to question seriously, even laugh at, the notion of God and faith; but I was also convinced that life is a mystery, for which evil and rationality do not render a sufficient account.

For a while I was content to keep the juggling act going. But now one of the balls had disappeared.

How long did I think this would last? How long did I think I could go on skirting the issues? How foolish I was for thinking no one noticed that I had begun to equivocate. Out of my snobbish, elitist training as a scholar I underestimated people's intelligence. And I overestimated my own. "This is not a course on what God said," I announced every year to first-year students who enrolled in my introductory course in the Old Testament; "this is a course on what the ancient Hebrews said God said." That was my pronouncement the first day of class every semester. But on Sundays I found myself standing before church audiences naked as a bark. "Speak, Lord, for your servants hear." Years of trying to wean students off the "why" questions had taken their toll on me. I thought I could convince them to be satisfied first with the "what" questions, hoping they would become as fascinated as I with "where" and "when"—which, of course, they didn't, since it's "why" that, in the first place, makes people stagger into sanctuaries, synagogues, and temples on holy days in search of burning bushes. I worked so hard at trying not to let my own beliefs spill over into my classroom that I didn't know how to talk any longer about God. Not with assurance. Not with confidence. God didn't drop by anymore. I'd spent so many years slaughtering other people's lambs that I looked up and found my own bleating and bleeding themselves. There's no way to take away other people's truth and have your own not be damaged in the process. I felt like the father who brought his epileptic son to Jesus, begging Jesus, "Have pity on us and help us." Jesus responded with a paradox: "All things are possible to him who believes." The father responded with a paradox of his own: "I believe; help my unbelief!" The only way through my dilemma, it seemed to me, was to confess that I didn't know anymore what to believe. That took more courage than I thought I could muster. But I managed. I stood in the pulpit trembling as I confessed that I didn't know how to believe in God anymore, and I stood before my academic colleagues admitting blushingly to twinges of faith I still had in such things as divine creation, supernatural healing, and the Resurrection. Confessing unbelief to believers and belief to unbelievers seemed to me at times the only sensible thing to do. I chose to preach through my unbelief and to teach my way back to belief.

Perhaps that is as honest as any one of us can ever aspire to be. To pray, to preach, to teach, and to hope *as though* we knew for sure that there is really someone on the other side of the door who heals, who hears, who answers. The issue in prayer is not to pray because we are certain, but to pray *because* we are *uncertain*. It is a risk where the risk itself is the outcome. I was never certain even when I believed. I was only certain that I believed. I was trying not to make a fool of myself more for what I knew than for what I hoped to gain.

The clock has just announced that it is 10:30 A.M. In thirty minutes, I must stand before a waiting congregation as though I believe. I have chosen a passage from a little-known prophet by the name of Habakkuk, whose cry to God is fitting to my heart: "O Lord, how shall I cry for help, and you will not listen?"

"The difference between you and me"—a friend's words to me long ago come to mind as I type the last sentence of the sermon—"is that you preach your questions, whereas I preach my answers." She was right. And she has the accolades to show for it. Her reputation as a preacher has far exceeded mine, both then and now.

A Chance Encounter

When you stop looking for something, you see it right in front of you.

ELEANOR COPPOLA

"So, how do I get in touch with my spiritual side?"

It's the kind of question that, as a minister and professor of Bible, I am asked at least a dozen times a month. But coming as it did one spring evening in Boston—from a rather successful, well-dressed, thirtyish African American female corporate executive as she deftly shifted the gears of her BMW with one hand and steered gracefully with the other hand—the question caught me by surprise. I sat quietly for a moment thinking how I'd heard drunks on bar stools broach the topic of spirituality with greater poise. The mixture of contempt and curiosity in her voice warned me that I probably wouldn't have anything to say that would satisfy my interrogator.

"It's obvious from the fact that you asked the question that you're already in touch with your spiritual side," I said, turning to look out the window at the dilapidated elegance of the Boston landscape. I secretly hoped she wouldn't pursue the conversation any further. I didn't feel like talking about God or spirituality—or anything that reminded me how long it had been since I had prayed. Besides, I wasn't up for the challenge of talking to this direct, efficient managerial type about subjects that defy tidy, reasonable prose, subjects like grace, prayer, faith, God, and mystery.

"You don't get it. I haven't been to church in years—except for when I attend funerals. And prayer . . . well, I doubt that

'God, I hope that check doesn't bounce' falls within the category of a real prayer." She laughed.

"This is prayer right here," I interjected a bit impatiently.

"Yeah, right. Well, it doesn't feel like prayer to me." She paused. "Besides, I hardly think my mother would be satisfied with this as prayer. If she had her way, I'd be somewhere on my knees, my head covered, with a rosary in my hand, mumbling something about mercy, sins, forgiveness and asking to be saved from eternal damnation."

"That's one kind of prayer. And there's a time and place for that kind of prayer, I suppose. This is another kind of prayer."

"You mean to tell me that I'm praying and don't even know it?" She laughed. "Maybe there's hope for me yet." She paused.

"What sense is there in praying if you don't believe in God?" Her tone had changed. She sounded pensive.

"You pray in order to believe," I answered.

"That sounds backwards to me. What's the sense in praying if you don't believe?"

"Sometimes you can't wait for your mind to catch up. Sometimes the heart has to take the initiative." I could feel her glancing at me out of the corner of her eye as she steered the sensitive machine down the street. I didn't trust myself to look directly at her.

It was her time to stare quietly ahead.

"Do you actually believe all that stuff about God, faith, prayer, and miracles you were talking about in front of everybody this morning?" she asked. There was more curiosity in her voice this time than contempt.

"Yes. Sort of." I stumbled. I hated myself for stumbling. This is no time for you to waver, I thought to myself. Not before a skeptic. She'll eat you alive. "Even when I don't, or can't, believe, I still believe that it's important to believe," I heard myself saying. "That's enough to keep me stammering prayers."

"You don't mean to tell me that you have doubts yourself?" she countered, taking her foot off the clutch a little too quickly. The car jerked forward, causing my head to fall back into the headrest. She turned her head slightly toward me with a smirk on her face.

My mind drew a blank. I felt trapped. Nothing slippery or profound came to mind.

"So, why the hell don't you just walk away from it and stop being a hypocrite?" The smugness in her voice was unmistakable.

"For the same reason I don't walk away from any of the myriad of things I've committed myself to. I don't want to live my life based solely on my feelings. Feelings change from one moment to the next. I don't walk away from my marriage just because I don't love my husband today. Eventually it returns."

"If you're lucky." She sneered. A ring was missing from the fourth finger of her left hand.

"Then I continue to pray until the belief returns," I answered, if only in my head. I can't remember what I said to her after that, nor do I remember today how the conversation three years ago concluded.

Ours was one of those chance encounters that leaves your soul spinning for years to come. It began as an unremarkable encounter, a chance meeting, an ordinary moment in time, as most encounters with the holy are on the surface. The young woman had a car and I needed a ride back to the hotel from the conference we both were attending. I had been the keynote speaker at a conference her company was giving on

spirituality and technology, and she had graciously consented
to drive me back to my hotel room. The conversation began
innocently with talk about schools, hometowns, family, mutual acquaintances; and without warning, and certainly without any prompting on my part as a minister, it turned to talk
about religion, God, the church, and finally prayer. My driver
was eager to show me up as a dimwitted, neoconservative,
right-wing, Bible-thumping Christian woman who couldn't
think for herself. She relished reminding me of every racist,
sexist, elitist, violent, abominable act done in the name of religion, and demanded that I try and defend the church. I could
not. Nor was I trying to. I was trying to talk to her about a
spiritual journey, when she was insistent that I explain every
immoral act that has been committed in the name of God. She
didn't hear me. But I heard me. It's one of those encounters
that the writer Frederick Buechner calls a saving mystery;
others have referred to it as a miracle of grace. I was content to
get out of the young executive's car with her thinking me a
dimwitted religious Southerner. After all, I was running short
on oracles. Still, I felt a bit ashamed that I hadn't defended the
faith more brilliantly. But then, my tongue always trips over itself when I'm called upon to talk about the least articulable of
matters—grace, prayer, faith, love, God, and mystery. I've
grown accustomed in this profession to stuttering.

I parted from the woman that spring evening permanently
changed by our chance encounter. What started as a typical
conversation between minister and skeptic ended rather routinely as a battle of wills, rhetoric, and of gods. There's no
denying that I clearly lost on behalf of whatever it was I was
supposed to be representing. But in losing the battle I won
something back within that probably wasn't worth anything
to anyone other than me. I remembered something I had for-

gotten. I remembered what prompted me to become a minister in the first place.

I couldn't resist peeping behind altars when I was little. Every time I had a chance to accompany my mother to the altar for Communion, I was always eager to peer behind the draped altar where the minister stood holding the elements. I knelt as I was instructed, but I just couldn't keep my eyes closed for fear that I might miss something. I was enthralled with the sights, sounds, and smells in front of me: the musty-smelling robes of the celebrants, the starched white linen cloth on the table, the glistening cup, the pieces of bread on the altar, the dizzying smell of wine, the stained cloth on the altar, the minister with fingers so fat they were bulging out of his wedding band.

I remembered in a speeding BMW in Boston one spring evening that whatever spirituality is, it is not something to be discovered. It is something to be recovered—something you misplace and recover a thousand times in a lifetime. Nor is belief in God, mystery, or prayer something one either possesses or doesn't. Rather, belief is something one tries continually to keep oneself open to, accessible to, or something one continually refuses to open oneself up to. The only difference between me, the fumbling, dimwitted minister who felt ill at ease talking about prayer, and the young corporate executive who couldn't talk about it without sneering was that I still wanted to remain open. Open to what? Open to the possibility that there was something more to life than my vanity, something more than what I could manipulate or grasp. As inadequate as I felt, and as far removed as I felt from the thing I ached most for that day, I wanted to remain open to the possibility that there was something nobler in life than what I could see or touch.

Sometimes we awaken to it through nature. Sometimes it comes to us through art, music, dance, or silence. Sometimes we are reminded of it by interacting with or observing children. Sometimes we happen upon it through chance encounters with strangers. And for a moment, we are smitten with the sublime. And then we lose it. We lose its scent, we can't make out its sound. Sometimes we stumble around for what feels like days, months, perhaps years, trying to recapture it—trying to pick back up the scent, trying to make out the sounds. But even though we find ourselves stumbling, we're onto something.

My effort to remain open to the sublime certainly doesn't make me any better than my corporate friend who pretends to have closed herself off from it. It only opens me to greater scrutiny and criticism when the most I can do is stammer and stutter about my losses and finds. As a minister, I find that people are apt to corner me all the time in hallways and public bathrooms and heap ashes upon my head for all the sins of religion. It comes with the job, but that day in a smoke-filled car driven by a woman who was ready to bludgeon me for every hurt she'd suffered at the hands of religion, the church, and God, I found myself thinking less of her anger and more of my own. I was angry at her for setting me up, angry at God for setting me up to be set up, and angry at myself for not recognizing a setup when I saw one. Our encounter marked me for life. Although I didn't know it at the time, our encounter would wind up being one of those mysteries that show up from time to time and leave me tripping over God. I guess you can say that I learned something about God. It's probably more the case that I learned something more about myself. I surely learned something about how God's presence presents itself to me. Just when I think I've stopped believing in God and can't figure out why I don't have the courage to do just what my driver encouraged me to do—walk away—something happens (a chance encounter, an overheard conversation, an old memory resurfacing) to bring new insight.

These luminous moments are otherwise quite unremarkable. They are otherwise ordinary moments, routine acts, commonplace occurrences, forgettable encounters. I have encountered inquisitors like the one in the BMW hundreds of times and have forgotten most of them. But at the edge of these otherwise everyday, commonplace, ordinary occasions comes an invitation by some irresistible force, by God, to come closer and listen more attentively. For example, sitting in a salon I overhear a conversation between strangers about a dispute on a job that brings tears to my eyes as I remember an old wound and an old friend I forgot to forgive a long time ago. Grace. I am sitting at an upscale restaurant eating Sunday brunch with ultramodern friends, and all of a sudden, for reasons I can't explain, when the conversation turns to grandmothers and Sunday dinners, the urge comes over me to bow my head and pray over the meatballs on my plate. Grace. Or I swerve to avoid hitting a child on a skateboard and at that precise moment I remember dreaming of swerving to avoid a child on a skateboard. I'm thumbing mindlessly through a magazine as my plane sits on the runway for two hours waiting clearance from the tower, and I read a travel writer's account of his trek through the Antarctic in search of the perfect cup of hot chocolate, and finally I've stumbled on an angle for the book I've been trying for months to write.

It is precisely moments like these that leave me tripping up into my purpose, staggering into some insight I desperately need, and backing up into God. On those rare and unforeseeable occasions, all of us have perceived the presence of a presence that leaves us incapable of speech, embarrassed by our ignorance, and wanting to take off our shoes.

I wish I could say that the female executive and I parted with her humbled and changed and me coming across as mystical and sagacious. But I can't. We parted much as we met, each too absorbed in her own thoughts to be of any help to the other. The conversation was clearly over. She had obviously said what she'd wanted all along to say. And I had obviously said all I knew to say. So why did I feel like such a failure as we drove the rest of the way to my hotel in silence? What should have been a fifteen-minute ride between office building and hotel had wound up taking more than an hour as the woman circled the city hurling one question after another at me. On the surface ours was an unremarkable meeting, albeit stormy—mundane, ordinary, unspectacular in its conclusion. But we parted that spring evening with me changed by our chance encounter. It had begun as a cordial meeting of strangers, one extending a helping hand to the other for what proved to be her own less than sincere reasons, but a gracious act nevertheless. It ended with the answer to an unspoken prayer.

Teach Us to Pray

Sometimes I think that just not thinking of oneself is a form of prayer.

BARBARA GRIZZUTI HARRISON

People who do not know how to pray, who do not have the discipline for meditation, and who have trouble believing in angelic appearances should not be given up on. Just because they can't bring themselves to meditate and to believe in God and angels doesn't mean they don't want to believe in the spiritual realm. More often, they just don't know how to believe. Nor do they know how to talk intelligently about their disbelief.

I, for one, believe. After all, I'm a minister. I believe in God. I pray, though not nearly as often as I ought. I can meditate, although I rarely have the time to do so. And I've glimpsed my share of epiphanies. But even I don't believe in the ways my slave ancestors did. Theirs was a much more sacramental world than mine. They knew an angel when they saw one. Not me. In fact, a whole year has almost passed and I can't remember anything that has happened this year that filled me with awe and wonder. Shame, yes. Disgust, frequently. Embarrassment aplenty. But hardly any awe and wonder. In fact, I can count on one hand the number of times I've felt compelled to kneel or fall prostrate without prompting or instruction.

I and those of my generation probably don't believe in God, in angels, and even in miracles the way our ancestors did. But that doesn't mean we don't want to believe. We just don't know how to talk genuinely about believing anymore.

We need a God who is not squeamish about disclosing the divine self in a thoroughly secular world and in the midst of ordinary daily existence, speaking to us through the noise of our hopeless routines and willing to touch us in our carnal places. We need a God who has more of a sense of humor than did our ancestors about what exactly constitutes prayer.

I Know Why Sarah Laughed

It takes me forever to say my prayers these days, but I don't care because this time around, I want to make sure God doesn't have to do any guesswork.

TERRY MCMILLAN

Some of us have placed ads in the personals for an angel who wears high-top sneakers and who does not stutter, someone who can keep up with our hectic pace and can think quick on her feet and doesn't need a lot of time to say what needs to be said. We are as desperate for a glimpse of the eternal as the next person, but we have neither the time, temperament, nor talent for meditation. We need revelations on the run. We need an angel who wears high-top sneakers, someone who can keep up with us on the treadmill or doesn't mind chatting from the passenger seat as we're stalled in rush hour traffic, someone who can pick up where she or he left off after calls come through on the cell phone, someone who isn't squeamish about talking to mothers while they nurse their babies. Those of us who are too klutzy to woo the holy need angels who can say what they have to say over the noise of screaming children and beeping microwave ovens. We do not have the time to decipher ponderous theological prose.

If God wishes to drop by my house, then she'd better bring her own broom. If she's got a good pair of lungs, she will have to be able to yell over the racket of the ten-year-old washer that lunges around the laundry room on the spin cycle. If God is trying to tell me something, what better way to chat and get my attention than by speaking through the stack of bills piled high on my desk? If she wants my attention, no better time to get it than when my daughter sleepwalks into our bedroom at 3 A.M. and I can't get back to sleep. If God is busy like me, however, and can't be in two places at one time, then I am placing an ad for an angel who is light on the feet, an angel who can keep up with my profoundly mundane, ordinary, uninspiring routine. Since I always have to run to the supermarket at least three times a week despite my best plans, I'd prefer one who when asked to pass me the long, thin maxi pads with wings will not think I'm making an oblique reference to an angel's body type.

Wanted: angels who don't stutter and who don't mind the sound of Rice Krispies crunching under their feet.

Simplicity

2 January 1987

Ambition, fame, and applause
have stolen from me the gift of simplicity:

the simple prayer
the simple hope
the simple thanksgiving
the simple faith.

So talented at what I do
as a writer, a minister, and a professor—
manipulating words, hiding behind phrases, exploiting traditions,
influencing opinions, crafting arguments, shaping ideas,
belittling some beliefs and extolling others,
drawing connections where there were none,
making a point—

I no longer know how to be prayerful.

Who am I?
Who is my self?

It is hard for me simply to pray,
to be myself, to say what I really mean,
to speak openly, vulnerably, plainly, innocently

to anyone,
especially to no one in particular.
Not to God.

To pray unimpressively, uncalculatedly, ineloquently,
honestly
an ordinary prayer,

Is no longer my self.

Without a thesaurus,
Without a point,

Without passion,
I don't know how to say what I want to say.

I don't know how to talk with no thought to changing your mind,
not caring to persuade you to see things differently,
not wondering if you get my point.

Thy will be done?
Then, why pray?

On the way to my purpose,

I looked around
and the simple prayer was gone.

The Longest Prayer

The purpose of prayer is not the same as the purpose of speech. The purpose of speech is to inform; the purpose of prayer is to partake.

ABRAHAM HESCHEL

Journal writing is for me a form of prayer. For more than twenty years now it has been my principal way to talk to God. When it began to hurt too much to pray, I started journaling as a substitute. Talking to paper was the only way I knew how to talk to God, and it proved to be an ideal form of prayer because it gave me a way to see what was going on in my heart.

Because journaling is not linear writing (I didn't have to be logical, neither did I have to have a point), when recording in a journal I was able to grope, stammer, and sniff my way to God. Prayer is work because so much time and energy is spent trying to talk myself into praying and trying to find the right words to. Journaling is a patient form of prayer because it doesn't require me to make sense, get to the point, or even to have a point. I can stalk a thought, circle a thought, abandon a thought and start over, double back to a thought, and repeat a thought again and again. Journaling let me strike out in prayer in whatever direction suited me and see where my heart and senses led me. Tolerant, receptive, friendly, uncritical, always willing to hear me out, and never put off by the fact that I repeated myself, my journal welcomed my stammering and patiently ushered me where I needed to go.

November 1982

It feels as though someone has flipped off the switch without telling me and I've been left to make my way in the dark. I keep hearing all these voices in my head, but I can't make them out. Run. Stop. Stand still. Scream. Over here. Over there. One more step. I've heeded each voice, but it doesn't feel as if I've gotten anywhere. I convince myself that I need to pray, but a part of me refuses to pray. I settle down to pray, but my heart is anything but settled. Why now? Why have I been hurled into this inner darkness when from all appearances on the outside things are dazzling and clear? I have a contract to publish my first book. Things are working out well on my new job. I'm settling into Nashville. Why now? When prayer should be easy, since there is so much to be thankful for, why do I think of ways to avoid doing it?

I didn't start off thinking of journaling as a way of praying when, in my twenties, I found myself developing a slight stutter. The stress and strain of working in the corporate world, the demand to prove myself, the pressure to produce-produce-produce, and the expectation that I would remain silent about what was happening to me undermined my self-confidence and left me speaking with a slight stutter noticeable perhaps to no one but me. Journaling, I told myself, gave me somewhere to tell the truth. I was out to regain my voice in the world. I needed a sounding board against which I could bounce my life. I needed a safe place to admit the things I dared not say out loud: that I was alone and afraid. Because it is such an intensely private conversation between myself and my self, journaling helped me to speak about my fantasies, my hopes, my ambitions, and my disappointments. Following the example of Anaïs Nin, Virginia Woolf, and Anne Frank, whose diaries I was reading the summer I bought my first journal, I started my journal fully expecting them to help me find my voice.

June 1979

Since I can't stand to hear myself pray, I've decided to buy this journal and see whether I can write my prayers out loud. I started writing as a way of hearing myself think, but pretty soon, by the fourth or fifth page, it's pretty clear that it's not me thinking but God who is whispering in my ear. But I don't know whether I'm up to hearing what God has to say. It may be something I don't want to hear. I'm afraid God might ask me to do something I don't want to do. Why am I so afraid that what God wants for me is sure to be nothing I'd want for myself? Since when did God become my declared enemy?

Not surprisingly, journal entries written during my twenties were filled with fantasies of rising to the top of whatever profession I was in at the time. Journaling helped me to keep up with the lives I was living as I was—just recently out of college and relocating from Boston to New York City—bounced around from job to job, from studio apartment to studio apartment, from church to church, from relationship to relationship, and from fantasy to fantasy. Journaling became a way for me to make sure that at least one person, or thing, knew the real me. Joan Didion's observation that writing was her way of keeping in contact with the many women who lived in her has always stuck with me. Journaling allowed me to stay on speaking terms with myself. And that self seemed always to be torn and ripped apart by competing claims.

May 1979

Lord, I don't want to be a minister. I'm not cut out to be warm, open, pious, and humble. Doesn't suit me. Besides, it sounds like a pretty boring life to me. So what if I've chucked my job with Merrill Lynch and have been working for two years full-time as a writer and haven't sold an article yet? I'm still a writer, sort of, kinda, I think. Find someone else. Just because I'm a praying woman doesn't make me a devout believer. What's wrong with following you from afar? I like the view from back here.

If prayer is a conversation, and I believe it is, it is not a conversation between two parties unfamiliar with each other. It is one between intimates, someone within talking with something or someone deeper within. It's a conversation between the inner selves. It seems that the real, the original, self, the self that continued to have something of God's original imprint, was always struggling to survive and be heard above the din of noise that insisted I give up bits and pieces of myself for family, friends, my career on Wall Street.

I started stuttering just about the same time God stopped speaking to me in thunderous tones. The lapse between epiphanies was becoming longer. I had attached myself to a little Baptist church in Brooklyn with a lively, earnest worshiping congregation, but it was becoming increasingly difficult to justify the injustices I was beginning to notice.

July 1979

Women bake the brown Communion bread and huddle in the corner of the church before service starts, pouring the Communion wine into tiny cups. The white linen tablecloth draping the Communion table is their doing. They worry over the stains in the cloth, probably staying up at night trying to remove them, not wanting anyone to think them lax about their sacred duties. But when the solemn time comes to stand, bless, and distribute the elements, women are nowhere to be found. Only men circle the table, well-meaning, earnest, praying men, who if made to open the table to women will, as Jesus observed, "deliver you up to be killed thinking they are doing the will of God."

Journaling gave me a place to pour out my disappointments—to look at them, to hear them out, to circle them and decide which ones I would just have to live with and which ones I would change. Journaling did not make me less interested in traditional forms of prayer, the closed-eyed, bended-knee, muttering-under-your-breath type of prayer. I knelt and wrote. Writing kept me honest when I knelt. I didn't panic if when I knelt nothing came to mind to say. I knew that there was more than one way to pray. The easiest thing in the world would have been to cease kneeling. But I didn't. My heart needed the practice.

"Absolute attention is prayer," writes Simone Weil. I'm grateful that journaling helped me to give God my absolute attention. Turning events over and over in my mind, poking around for the meaning of things, reliving conversations, pulling bits and pieces of dreams and experiences together, doubling back and returning to old wounds in the hopes of making my peace with them and moving on became the only way I knew to pray. "Stalking epiphanies" is the way I came to refer to all this sniffing around my soul started doing. I could pray long, repetitious, endless, meandering, yearlong, decade-long prayers to God in my journal and not worry about prolonged church services bruising my knees. Since prayer requires us to be present to God, and because journaling is a spontaneous act, not premeditative in the way that writing a book or organizing a speech is, then journaling showed God, I hope, that I was attentive and listening. Attentive and listening—important ingredients to prayer, don't you think? But I'm not always certain that God spoke back to me in my journaling.

From time to time (when I'm feeling brave) I take some volumes down from the shelf to reread, and I am embarrassed by what I come across in them. How *in one lifetime* can any one person be so catty, petty, snobbish, narrow minded, prejudiced, intolerant, manipulative, unforgiving, and sometimes downright mean spirited? Who can blame God for shutting down? I sometimes think upon reading old journals. It's a wonder I didn't shut down on myself. But God didn't shut down. In fact, the more I raved, the more likely I was eventually to be stopped dead in my tracks. From time to time angels slammed me to the mat to make me notice what was happening in my life. Every now and then, in between the muck and mire, the petty outbursts, the trivial complaints, the out-of-control rage, a burst of light came through. An insight, a revelation, a wild and crazy grace, a glimpse of eternity inserts itself upon the pages of my journal that leaves me hushed. I begin noticing patterns, making connections, and sneak up on purposes larger than my own narrow preoccupations. Angels laughing, perhaps? I can't be sure. All I know is that these entries pop up unexpectedly in my journal, like weeds sprouting up between cracked concrete, offering me epiphanies, revelations, insights, ways to let go, to move on, to learn, to heal, to understand, and to be thankful.

January 1994

Because I grew up in a home of abuse and addiction, silence feels like rejection to me. Quiet was a welcome. But silence was the way we ignored each other, punished each other, protected each other from outsiders, and pretended not to notice what was going on. Silence was the weapon of fathers and mothers. And slowly it became the weapon of their children. And so, O God, your refusal to scream, to stomp, and yell makes me think you're off somewhere pondering a better way to fell me. Your silence makes me think you're penalizing me for not doing what you demanded. Your silence feels like you're ignoring me. Your silence feels as though you're deliberately keeping me out of the loop. But you're not my father and not my mother, are you? Then who are you who use silence to be intimate rather than to push away?

By dusting off and rereading my journals, I get to relive the past and to retrace the hand of blessing in it. I get to relive the past and to redeem it. I get to relive it and to reinterpret the parts that once felt unsurvivable. More important, through my journals I get to play back God's voice. I get to pick up on things I probably missed before. I get to see through the passing of time—weeks, months, years later—what was oftentimes too hard to see before. Patterns begin to appear. I get to see the patterns that were always there but that, for whatever reason, I ignored: recurring patterns, repeated cycles, and persistent motifs of curses and blessings, lamentations and praise, hurt and healing. To my horror, I discover how little I've changed over the years. Some things continue to annoy me. (For instance, I still dislike being baited on my views so someone can evaluate my political or theological correctness on an issue. Grrrrrrr.) On a positive note, I'm glad to see that there are some things I still remain true to—I'm still inclined to bet the farm on the underdog. I've changed so little and yet changed so much. I still rant and rave, but for days rather than for weeks. I still hurt, but not for as long. And I forgive quicker.

I still complain that God is silent. But I'm not as frightened of the silence as I once was. Silence is not quickly mistaken for rejection anymore. Silence is just that, silence—a different way of getting me to listen and pay attention. And lest I pretend to be completely unlike that twenty-two-year-old girl of former days, I still long for the loud, thunderous yesses (I think) I heard when I was a teenager and young adult. As stressful as being an adult is sometimes, I could stand a rousing, foot-stomping, exuberant religious experience at this moment to perk up my spirits. I've been to the real world and it's not all it's cracked up to be.

God used journaling to wean me off the thunder. I had to pay attention to the wind, as invisible, ephemeral, and unpre-

dictable as it is. I had to draw connections, sniff out the purpose of things, weave and bob around meaning, and chase
down healing.

Twenty years ago my journals consisted of reams and
reams of longing and lust—boredom, restlessness, unfulfilled
dreams, broken promises, haunting nightmares, books I
wanted to write, money I wanted to make, friendships that
kept me on edge, men I wanted to love me. Twenty years later
I am absorbed with about pretty much the same things (except it's only one man, my husband, whom I'm trying to help
learn how to love me). Admittedly, I'm not always proud of
my prayers and private conversations with God. Nonetheless
I am grateful to be able to look back over some of the longest
prayers imaginable. They are my stutters before the holy. I
shudder to think of my journals falling into the wrong
hands—say, someone who might mistake them for truth.

Still, I've learned some things from this long affair with
written prayers. For one thing, sometimes you have to pray
the prayers you can until you can pray the prayer you want.
Second, prayer is not so much learning to write or talk to
someone or some presence outside yourself as becoming
mindful of a conversation already taking place deep inside.

An Old Self
19 September 1979

*What will ultimately happen to me? Will I ever break through
this haze blanketing my spirit? How much depends upon me?
How much rests upon God, and how much remains with me to
make of my life what it will be? It's tough being twenty-five years
old. I ask myself these questions—no, badger myself with these
questions—as I watch myself sink daily in a more desperate state.*

No job. No prospect of a job. No desire for a job. No idea what I want to do. Not depression but despair. Depression is so passive. Despair sounds better. It implies a struggle of some sort, some kind of action.

It's a season ripe for miracles. But who wants to live her life on miracles? Miracles are fickle, unreliable, unpredictable. I don't think I want to place my peace of mind in the hands of miracles. Is that the way to describe divine intervention, by talking about miracles? Is divine intervention my only help? Or will I have to rescue myself?

I'm ashamed of the shambles of my life, so much that I hesitate to enumerate the details here. They sound the same as they were a few years back, two months back. I feel as if I've left only to return to the same spot, facing the same dark tunnel.

Yesterday I asked for a blessing.

Today I pray for a sign.

Tomorrow I will look for a miracle.

Ordinary Time

The incredible gift of the ordinary! Glory comes streaming from the table of daily life.

MACRINA WIEDERKEHR

For more than seven months out of the year, the human spirit is left to scramble and fend for itself. Life must be lived outside the feasts and fasts of the Christian calendar, and believers are expected to figure out for themselves how to calibrate and celebrate mystery. This period, referred to in the Orthodox, Anglican, and Roman traditions as "ordinary time," comprises the longest portion of the liturgical calendar, referring as it does to the almost thirty weeks in the year where no particular mystery of Christ is celebrated. The inference is that the human heart can only take so much celebration before it recoils with dread. For seven months we are shorn of high holy days and left dependent upon the routine of worship, prayer, the Eucharist, and our own imaginative designs to mediate God. It is the period between Christmas and Lent, and it picks back up again after Pentecost and continues until Advent. It distinguishes itself as the no-particular-reason interval in the liturgical calendar. The Christological festivals are past. The mystery is presumably over. The ordinary resumes. And believing hearts are left to grapple for themselves with the silence of God. Or so it seems, that God is silent. Perhaps it's humans who are speechless for those thirty weeks.

Deep in the religious instinct is the desire to order time. The liturgical calendar regulates time according to holy days and seasons in an effort to help believing hearts peer into mystery. For those requiring more finely tuned calibrations, the Roman church has broken the day into canonical hours, which are to be understood as natural rhythms in which one might live consciously and responsively throughout the stages of the day. The belief is that as we become more deeply sensitive to the nuances of time, we become more available to the present moment. That is the way it's supposed to work. But it rarely works out that way. The hurried, harried character of our modern existence sees to it that there are plenty of hours and days when we forget completely about how really precious the present is and how finite is our existence. We take life for granted and we fail to cultivate an appreciation for what is truly holy. Without feasts, fasts, religious observances, and sacred holidays to remind us to pause and take inventory, seven months is a long time to be expected to figure things out for ourselves.

When, in seminary, I first learned about ordinary time, I was intrigued. Belonging as I have most of my life to what some might call "low church" traditions, where emphasis is less on liturgy and more on the gathered congregation as the manifestation of the visible Christ, I had no language available for talking about those times when God felt silent. Reading an old journal entry of mine dated August 11, 1987, my eyes fell upon these words: "I'm not mad at God; I just don't have anything to say to God." Looking back on this period of my life, when I was still in school and trying to finish a dissertation, trying to get a job, and had recently had my heart crushed by unreciprocated love, I felt alienated from God's affection. As far as I was concerned, God became silent first. My silence was in response to God's silence. "I talk to people who talk to me," I wrote further in my journal, trying to justify myself. I was indignant at God's silence, but I was also afraid of it. I wondered what I had done. I tell myself that if ordinary time had been a part of my religious psyche, I might have been spared blaming myself for years when my spiritual journey was lackluster and God felt far away. I could have relaxed in the notion that God's silence needn't mean God's absence, that for the believing heart, as James Carse wrote, "the silence of God . . . is precisely the way God is present." As a concession to the ruthlessly independent side of human beings and their need to figure things out for themselves, the church relaxes its imperial control and gives individuals the opportunity to come up with their own devices for communicating with the holy.

My third grade teacher, Miss Susie Mae Skinner, taught sign language to her elementary school class. Actually, we learned only the alphabet, but it was enough to provide me a way to endure the loneliness of childhood. Despite having a sister and three brothers, I was a very private, introspective child growing up, who spent much of her time talking and entertaining her imaginary friends. Since it seemed that the *Father Knows Best* home life was never going to be mine in real life, I determined to fashion one for myself in my head. Learning to sign gave me a way to increase the size of the family that lived in my head and allowed some characters to gain a unique voice over domestic scenarios I created in my mind. As soon as I mastered the alphabet I sat for hours at my desk and in my bedroom signing and talking to myself. So taken was I with this new skill that I began to sign almost reflexively words, phrases, and conversations I overheard wherever I went. Members of my (real) family began noticing my odd behavior, the fact that my fingers were constantly moving, along with my lips, and that I could sit for hours signing as I sat watching television, ate dinner at the table, bathed in the tub, or sat alone in my room. My father was afraid of what was happening to me and demanded that I stop. At least once he slapped me to get me to stop and to get me to notice what I was doing.

But I didn't know how to stop signing. I want to say that I was fascinated with being able to make words with my fingers, even though I didn't know one deaf-mute. I was delighted to be able to talk to the silence with my fingers. But thinking back on that time in my life and recalling all the loneliness I felt as a third-grader, I think I was grateful to Miss Skinner for giving me a way to have private conversations with myself.

She gave me a way to live with the loneliness and silence that were choking away at my little eight-year-old heart. Signing made the world less frightening and less silent. And while I'm sure I could have improved my skills had there been someone to sign back to me, I was grateful nevertheless for an art form, a discipline, a creative venue for the long intervals of loneliness and quiet that filled my existence.

Ordinary time. The pause between speech. The "lull in the rhythm of time," as Howard Thurman describes it. Another way to think about it is to compare the liturgical interval known as ordinary time with the time-out period caretakers sometimes must impose on headstrong toddlers. Time-outs are for the precious little souls that need a period of time to compose themselves, gather their thoughts, calm down, think about what they are doing, and find their way back into the give-and-take of intimacy.

Perhaps God is not silent but rather is waiting—waiting for human beings to gather their thoughts, compose themselves, regain their speech, and find their way back into the give-and-take of intimacy with God. After all the grand reenactments of divine presence in the festivals of Advent, Christmas, Lent, Easter, and Pentecost have ceased, God awaits our finding ways to carve sentences out of the silence. It is a creative waiting on the part of the divine, a sort of "hearing us into speech." No longer relying upon the grand booming rhythms of the holy festivals to disclose the divine self, the Eternal One now gestures and prods us into speech through the quiet—but oftentimes disquietude—of our routine, ordinary existence. As with most great communicators, God knows that the point of silence and the pause between sentences is not to give the audience the chance to fill the silence with empty babbling but to help create more depth to the conversation.

Blessed Quietness

Prayer begins where expression ends.

ABRAHAM HESCHEL

Reading about prayer is the closest sometimes you can bring yourself to pray. Often it hurts too much to pray. Sometimes the words get in the way. Other times you run out of words. Occasionally you find yourself in a season when prayer is impossible. You want to pray but your soul is engulfed in silence. It is such a radical change from an earlier period, when prayer was easy. The challenge is to find new ways to pray. Sometimes the most effective prayers are the ones that never get formulated into words.

One day after I had finished reading to my daughter for what felt like the 129th time in 130 days her favorite bedtime story (it's the one about a newly hatched bird who falls from his nest in search of a mother who has gone off to comb the countryside for food to feed her baby bird), I reminded my daughter that it was time for her to say her prayers and go to sleep. She lay quiet, with her thumb in her mouth, and stared intently into my face. Interpreting her stillness as yet another tactic devised by the ingenious mind of a toddler to outwit her mother and to get Mommy to postpone turning off the lights for fifteen more minutes, I stiffened to show my authority. "Come on, Savannah. Let's say our prayers and go to sleep," I said, closing the book and resting it on her nightstand.

"I prayed already, Mommy." She snatched the book from the nightstand and pretended to read it. She avoided my eyes and stared intently down at the pages, pretending to read it. The book was upside down in her hands.

With mock indignation I removed the book gently from her clutch, and holding her sheets up, I motioned for her to slide down underneath.

"When did you pray, Savannah?" I asked.

"I prayed to the quiet, Mommy," she said, sliding down in the sheets.

"Oh?" I replied skeptically.

She turned her back to me and before putting her thumb in her mouth she said, "When you were turning the pages, Mommy, I was praying to the quiet."

I didn't demand that my daughter pray twice that evening. Learning to pray to the quiet while pages are turning and life is transitioning and the story muddles along would be talent enough to get her through decades of darkness. Besides, just because I didn't hear her pray didn't mean that God didn't hear her pray.

Growing up as I did in a large, loud, raucous family and belonging to a robust little Pentecostal church of people who came weekly in the hopes of witnessing some tangible, extraordinary assurance of God, I could have used more talk about the times when God is perfectly silent. Given the emphasis we placed on public, visible, supernatural signs of visitations from the holy that manifested themselves in the form of tongue speaking, ecstatic worship, feverish dance, romping, singing, or an unquenchable flow of tears, the inference was that the more desperate the need, the more spectacular would be God's response. Such inferences impaired me later. There was hardly any talk in my church about the sanctity of inarticulable prayers. And I don't believe anyone would have been courageous or honest enough to admit that sometimes the closest we can come to praying is simply staring into space. Nor do I recall any talk about the possibility of God failing to respond to our outcries. What use would such a God be to oppressed people? And so I have spent what seems now to be a lifetime trying to cultivate an appreciation for quiet praise. I have spent what seems now to be a lifetime trying to come up with a theology of silence. I have spent a decade now trying not to feel compelled to fill the silence as the pages turned. There is in silence music to be heard, I am told. For every note chosen, there are others not played—another sound, another melody, another message that waits to be heard. Trust the quiet to bear your prayers, I tell myself. I've spent a lifetime addicted to noise. And now that I'm smack in the midst of a long, still quiet, where I'm no longer sure how to recognize God's voice, I am terrified. "Pray to the quiet," my daughter teaches me. Stick my thumb in my mouth, as she does, and pray to the quiet.

Saint Fallow

Command your soul to be still.

JESSICA KENDALL INGRAM

I have learned a lot from gardening, though not as much as I might learn if I could convince myself to venture outdoors to the vacant patch of dirt in my front yard. I've tried to convince myself to poke around outside with the new trowel and seed planter that lie idly against my garage wall. But I can't bring myself to do it. I can't bear the thought of kneeling in the dirt in my yard. My husband teases that I don't want to ruin my French manicure. But I'm tougher than that, I want to believe. I'm just not tough enough to face snakes. That's right, snakes. Slimy reptiles have lately turned up in my neighbors' driveways and garages, and near their retaining walls. (I've seen two on the street, but I can't be sure since I passed out before getting a very good glance at them.)

Set as our new development is on a rolling Nashville hill, the back of my house looks out over the south side of the city with a view of the downtown skyline. But the front of my house, where the vacant patch of dirt sits, faces a steeper, though as yet underdeveloped, thicket of woodlands. Rabbits, deer, and raccoons come down during dry months from the hill in search of water and better vegetation. Snakes crawl down on more frequent occasions in search of only God knows what.

One of the first lessons I learned from *not* gardening in my yard is how very much a fundamentalist I am at heart when it comes to interpreting parts of scripture. Despite all that I learned while working on a doctorate degree in the history of biblical interpretation, one verse remains, to my thinking, straight from the mouth of God: "Now the serpent was the most subtle of any of the wild animals the Lord God had made." As they say among conservative Bible-believing Christians: "God said it. I believe it. That settles it."

Say what you will about parts of the Bible straining the imagination, Genesis comes as close to the eternal, timeless, universal truth as I have ever heard it told. Snakes are menacing, crafty, slimy, and are to be avoided at all costs—whether they are long ones, short ones, green ones, spotted ones, garden snakes, or water snakes. And creation never intended for me, a woman, to have any dealings with snakes, I remind my husband, the pastor.

"Says so in Genesis," I tell him, pointing to the verse. " 'I will place enmity between you [serpent] and the woman,' says God," I remind him. My fate with snakes is sealed. No sense fighting it.

When we were building our home I mapped out in my head where I wanted to plant the irises, coreopsis, caladium, astilbe, tulips, daffodils (just beneath the dining room window), the black-eyed Susans (outside my study window), and the roses (outside my daughter's window). I visited nurseries throughout the city, bought books on gardening, sent off for bulbs, and had a friend who does landscaping come over and give me a few tips on gardening. But that was before I knew about the snakes. "Just little garden snakes," my neighbor teased me. So was the snake in Genesis. See what damage it did. The moment I found out about the snakes I took my expensive new trowel, my designer gardener gloves, and my fancy gardening bench and propped them up in the garage. Whatever lessons about mystery awaited me by way of gardening would have to be taught from a pot. I gave up my fantasy of becoming another May Sarton, poet and devoted gardener. Now, there was a woman knew how to squeeze mystery out of a garden. But I was no May Sarton. Fine with me. For even now as the winter approaches and everything outside is brown and drooping except the pansies, I look around my house and am stupefied by the wonder of revelations that have come to me through rooms of potted plants.

Which brings me to the second and most important lesson I have learned from gardening indoors and *not* gardening outdoors.

Plants go through a dormant period. Now, this may be obvious to the rocket scientist and the accomplished gardener. And it may sound familiar and reasonable to the informed mind. But it took me two winters of living with plants to learn this lesson. Plants need their nap. They need rest from growing. For two winters I couldn't figure out why virtually every plant in my house all but died, including the hardiest, reputedly most forgiving, any-idiot-can-grow-this-plant philodendrons. What didn't die crawled into spring looking scraggly, withered, and brown, gagging from my winter ministerings. Plain and simple: I watered and fertilized my plants in the winter as much as I had done in the summer's sweltering heat. It's an easy temptation to fall prey to when plants are indoors, when everywhere you turn in your house a plant is dangling on a ledge and a faucet is nearby. Let's just say that I thought I was being a caring, attentive caretaker.

It never dawned on me that just as I cut back on my water intake during the winter, likewise my plants could do without all that internal excitement. In this world of stimulation addicts and work junkies, "rest does need a saint," says one gardening expert. For two winters I watered and fertilized plants in my house, expecting them to perform in the winter months as they did in the summer months, wondering why they were drooping and turning brown instead of bursting with color and texture. It took nearly killing all of them for me to experience an epiphany of sorts. My potted friends were teaching me that it's all right to slow down, to stifle the stimulation, to rest. Sometimes the best course of action is to do nothing. That's right. Sleep on it. Rest. Lie low. Cool it. Chill out, as the young might say. Allow the body to catch up with the mind. Or better yet, let the body gear *down* to the soul's pace. Sleeping on it needn't be taken as a sign of indecisiveness and lack of ambition. Sleep is the only time most of us have solitude. And solitude is what winter forces most upon us.

There is a difference between aloneness and loneliness, just as there is a difference between fallowness and barrenness. If left unchecked, one may lead to the other; but both solitude and the season of fallowness can be seen as a "creative death" (using Sarton's phrase) or "creative waiting" (so says Molly Peacock) where loneliness and barrenness are like a bottomless void that refuses to be filled. Nothing can fill it and nothing should be forced to do so. Relax in the fallowness, I tell myself, and let it do its work. "Every flower holds the whole mystery in its short cycle," May Sarton wrote once, "and in the garden we are never far away from death, the fertilizing, good, *creative* death."

Constant fatigue may be a sign of a season of fallowness. I can't write these days beyond the incoherent ramblings I record in my journal. I want to write. I need to write. My reputation as an academic depends upon my writing articles and books. Without a pulpit, my work depends upon my writing. But nothing comes. Saint Fallow, I fear, has visited my soul. Nothing coherent comes to mind. Nothing publishable comes across my computer screen. I feel fatigued. And yet, I contracted to meet a publisher's deadline this month, never suspecting that the deadline might fall during the feast of Saint Fallow, when I can't think of anything to say. I wish I could do as the bear does and crawl in a hole and hibernate when it's cold and barren outside, but life does not permit human beings such luxuries. I have to produce when I should be sleeping.

There arrives a third mystery from gardening indoors. As winter chases us indoors, we discover that some plants strut and prance during this season. African violets bloom constantly. Peace lilies send up white shoots about this time. A little growth is still left in the croton my Trinidadian husband brought back from his mother's front yard back in La Romain. Although the jade plant in my study grows infuriatingly slow and will probably not grow more than four feet tall (so I am told), it never loses its fleshy, emerald green color even in the dead of winter, when outdoor relatives are dying back. The point here is that not everything goes into hibernation during the winter. While virtually everything requires less watering and less fertilization now, still, some plants thrive in cooler temperatures. Some seem to thrive on neglect, like my lush pothos. But it took two winters of watering when I should have been observing to discover this.

Not having the luxury to withdraw into a cave of solitude, free of deadlines and obligations, I learn to confine my work to the things that thrive on winter conditions. Only certain kinds of books get written in the winter. These are the ones that require a considerable amount of rest and sleeping on it. Some of my better sermons on pain, death, loss, the mystery of suffering, and the silence of God were born when I was in the throes of wrestling with Saint Fallow. Realizing that it's impossible to be in season all the time, I find it easier simply to let the season dictate what gets done and what doesn't. Unfortunately, however, the seasons of the soul do not always coincide with the seasons of the year. It's not unusual to be in the middle of the South's sweltering humid heat and experience a deep freeze gripping me within. Similarly, I'm in no mood to stand in the long lines at Disney World during the summer, but despite a book deadline I cannot get out of walking alongside my daughter as she rides her bike back and forth on the street on late summer evenings. The walk gives me time to think. When I'm forced inside for days for the annual Nashville ice storm, I can draw from the renewed zest I feel inside me to hole up in my study and write a theology of hope as my next academic writing project.

For now I content myself with God speaking to me through plants. Or more accurately, I accept the fact that God used my fear of snakes to force me indoors, where the mystery of dying and renewal is learned in commodious doses of potting soil. I don't feel cheated for choosing to retreat indoors. I've had my share of failures indoors and learned from them: eliminate the parasites and don't force growth where there is none. I've also learned from my share of accomplishments: preparation is everything and patience is a virtue. But unlike outdoor gardeners, I've learned my lessons free from bee stings, sunburn, backaches, and—God forbid—menacing snakes underfoot. I'm happy to study nature indoors. I'm thankful to snakes, I suppose, although I'll never say that to one.

Come Sunday

Every day will be Sunday, and the Sabbath will have no end.

NEGRO SPIRITUAL

Once upon a time Sunday was a special day, a holy day, a day different from the other six days of the week. This was back before malls were ubiquitous and when shopkeepers after six days of receipts thought nothing of locking up Saturday in late afternoon and not opening their shop doors again until Monday morning. This was a time when colored people like those I grew up with still believed that it was enough to spend six days a week trying to eke out a living, worrying about whether you were ahead or behind, fretting over the future, despairing over whether life would ever get better for coloreds. Six days of worrying were enough. The Sabbath was the Lord's Day, a momentary cease-fire in our ongoing struggle to survive and an opportunity to surrender ourselves to the rest only God offered. Come Sunday, we set aside our worries about the mundane and renewed our love affair with eternity.

It wasn't until I was grown up, with a family of my own, that I understood the Sabbath to be the gift it was meant to be. While I chafed as a child at its don'ts, can'ts, mustn'ts, and don't-even-think-about-its, I miss today the discipline it imposed upon me and the demands it made on me. I miss living around people who keep me accountable to sacred moments. Never mind that we took turns failing to adhere strictly to the canonical prohibitions related to Sabbath observance. After all, who could anticipate all the things that might go wrong with Sunday dinner? Who would imagine all the things that could and did go awry when trying to get little ones ready for church? Who could say for sure whether that old car in the driveway would start on cold Sunday mornings? Whether you found that (despite your best planning) you simply had to dash to the store on Sunday afternoon for extra tea bags, or that your son's pants required pressing before church, or that the car needed to be jump-started, every Sabbath infraction was always done in a chorus of "Lord, have mercy on my soul" and "Do, Jesus" to make perfectly clear to God that despite the idealism of the fourth commandment, you, the violator, simply did not live in a perfect world.

Our working-class hearts were ultimately fixed on one thing alone. Sunday held out to us the promise that we might enter our tiny rough-hewn sanctuary and find sanctity and blessing from a week of loss and indignities. Remembering the Sabbath where I grew up involved delighting oneself for a full twenty-four hours, ultimately in good company, with fine clothes and choice meals. The Sabbath allowed us to mend our tattered lives and restore dignity to our souls. We rested by removing ourselves from the mundane sphere of secular toil and giving ourselves over fully to the divine dimension, where in God's presence one found "rest" (paradoxically) not in stillness and in repose but in more labor—a different kind of labor, however. We sang, waved, cried, shouted, and when we felt led to do so, danced as a way of restoring dignity to our bodies as well. We used our bodies to help celebrate God's gift of the Sabbath. For the Sabbath meant more than withdrawal from labor and activity. It meant to consciously enter into a realm of tranquillity and praise.

After a week of the body toiling away in inane work and the spirit being assaulted with insult and loss, Sunday was set aside to recultivate the soul's appreciation for beauty, truth, love, and eternity. It was as though time stood still on Sunday. It was a day of magic. Time was different; life was different; the very air we breathed was, it seemed, different on Sunday. We ate together as a family. We went for drives in the country as a family. Husbands and wives called a halt to their bickering on Sunday and spoke in hushed tones in front of children. Even the drunks in the neighborhood quit drinking on Sunday, and the prostitutes were grateful for a day to sleep in. It was also the one day Big Mama, my grandmama, made the most supreme sacrifice of all, which was to refrain from dipping snuff.

In contrast to the magic of Sabbaths past, I am afraid that

Sunday at my house as an adult feels like every other day of the week. We all get up rushing. We run, iron, fuss, grab a carton of juice with a straw attached to it, break the speed limits to get to church, swearing at other drivers, and murmur because the parking lot is full, which means we won't get to sit in our favorite seat; and we are glad that when we get home everyone has his or her own activities, his or her own bedroom, and his or her own car to entertain himself or herself. Those of us with active families look forward to the Sabbath as a time to take a break both from our weeklong jobs and from the give-and-take of family and intimacy. Instead of the Sabbath being a time to relax and mend relationships, it offers many of us the opportunity we need to excuse ourselves from interacting with family, friends, and even God. I have chosen, to my own detriment, vegetating over contemplating, and isolation over association.

Somewhere between girlhood and postmodern womanhood, I stopped believing in magic. I stopped keeping the Sabbath. I stopped believing in eternity. I ceased seeing the wisdom in restraint. After a while, anything goes, I came to believe. I miss having a weekly alarm sounded to remind me to stop, rest, start anew, yield to a different pace. Taken with the notion that I was free to worship or not worship, believe or not believe, pray or not pray whenever I wanted, I bowed to very little. Devoid of a sacramental universe, I, like others in my generation, was left to decide for myself when and where and whether I rested, prayed, or worshiped God.

I didn't just stop observing the Sabbath, however. I stopped believing in things being holy. I crossed a boundary. I crossed a boundary, and that would forever brand me a sensible person, a thoroughly modern sophisticated woman, an intelligent human being, and a product of my upper-class educational background. I threw off any childhood superstitions I harbored in my heart and came to believe that Sunday was just like any other day of the week; and so it really was all right to go to brunch with friends, go to the movies, attend an aerobics class, iron, cook, grade papers, mow the grass, or sweep leaves off the driveway on Sunday. I found myself becoming increasingly addicted to toil. There was always something to do, especially on Sunday.

The phone rings at 11:34 P.M., and it's my girlfriend calling from Seattle, still in her office (at 9:34 P.M.) preparing briefs, answering correspondence, and billing customers.

"Why didn't you answer my E-mail yesterday?" she balks when I answer the phone.

"Yesterday was Sunday," I reply.

"And what's your point?" she hurls back. She's right. With beepers, faxes, and electronic mail operating all the time, there's no reason not to be *available* to work even on the Lord's Day. Nothing is ever closed anymore on the Lord's Day, and no one is ever *off* on the Lord's Day. My friend in Seattle runs back and forth between her office and church on Sunday. The boundary between sacred time and mundane time becomes blurred.

Nothing happened on the outside to mark this internal change, of course, for either her or me. Contrary to my grandmother's warning, God did not strike me dead when I sent off a fax on Sunday. I didn't get leprosy, and my hair and teeth didn't inexplicably fall out. Breaking the Sabbath became easier, and soon there was nothing to prevent me from doing so and justifying it to myself. I managed to sever my ties to a world filled in some ways with harmless superstitious beliefs, and that was good. But as silly, nonsensical, and naive as those beliefs were (and some of them still are), remembering the Sabbath was comforting.

Observing the care with which the adults around us took to refrain on Sunday from any hint of work and toil was supposed to reinforce certain notions about the world in the psyches of us children. It was to teach us things about order, boundaries, and discipline. Knowing that the Sabbath was just around the corner made demands upon us and disciplined us in certain directions. The Sabbath demanded that we *do* better, even if we weren't intrinsically any better human beings on Sunday than we were on Saturday. It reminded us what we could be. It gave us something to aim for—peace, tranquillity, love, Paradise, eternity, a vision of heaven on earth. It forced us to create boundaries. It forced us to remember that we would never have everything we wanted and would never finish the work of righting all the wrongs of the world. We had to accept our limitation and enjoy this one moment that was ours. We were forced to admit that the world really could survive without our constant tinkering and fixing. These were the lessons of the Sabbath when I was a child.

My Jewish and Adventist friends tease me that the reason I'm constantly tired and am never refreshed after Sunday is that I celebrate the Sabbath on the wrong day. Originally beginning at dusk on Friday and extending until dusk on Saturday, the Sabbath was changed from Saturday to Sunday when Christians, following the edict of Constantine (as well as others, once Christianity became the official religion of the Roman and Byzantine empires), were eager to distinguish the Christian Sabbath from the Jewish Sabbath. Whether it's celebrated on Saturday or on Sunday, it was intended as a gift from God, argued the sixth-century B.C.E. Jewish priests living in Babylon.

Borrowing from the Babylonian seven-day cycle, the Jewish priests fixed on to the Sabbath as a way to equalize rela-

tions between rich and poor, slave and free, employer and em-
ployee, parents and children, humans and animals, friends
and stranger alike by reminding us all of our universal need
for rest. The priests were correct: labor takes its toil on the la-
borer. It dulls the soul. It saps our emotions. It drains the
senses. It distorts our vision. Instead of giving us the security
we long after, it makes us greedy and anxious that we still
don't have enough. Above all, work and labor make us begin
to measure life according to *things.* Whether they are the objects we accumulate over a certain amount of time or the accomplishments we can show for how we used our time,
things, not life, become what is important. We forget how sacred time itself is until we have so very little of it left.

The Lord's Day allows us to bring our souls, our emotions, our senses, our vision, and even our bodies back to God
so that God might remember our tattered, broken selves and
put our priorities back in order. The Sabbath makes sure we
have the time to do what's really important and be with those
we really care about.

I miss the Sabbath of my childhood. I miss believing in the
holiness of time. I miss believing there was a day when time
stood still. There's virtually little in this culture, and hardly
anything in my adult comings and goings, to serve as a timely
reminder of how precious time really is, to remind me of sacred moments. No one I know observes the Sabbath the way
we did when I was a child; that includes many of the obser-
vant Jews and Adventists who are friends. Both groups of
friends enthusiastically adhere to the rules and traditions of
Sabbath worship, as far as I can tell, but neither holds out any
promise or welcome to me as a non-Jew and non-Adventist
that the Sabbath is a gift from God to *everyone,* whether believer or nonbeliever. This is the Sabbath I miss.

Chapter Two

The Mystery of Ministry

And the Word Became Flesh

Stories are medicine.

CLARISSA PINKOLA ESTES

The mystic and philosopher Howard Thurman tells the story of his grandmother, an ex-slave and a deeply devout woman, who never learned to read the Bible she grew so deeply to love. Her inability to read left her dependent upon others to read the Bible for her, but not dependent upon others to tell her what was God's word and what was not. She knew God's voice when she heard it. The Bible was to be cherished, as far as she was concerned, but it was not to go unscrutinized. What she heard and loved in the Bible, she insisted be read again and again. What she found obnoxious, she refused to hear. Thurman described the story of having to read the Bible out loud to his grandmother two or three times a week. She was picky about the portions of scripture she wanted to hear read. The psalms were a must; portions of Isaiah were welcome, as was the gospel again and again. But never the epistles of Paul, except (at long intervals) the thirteenth chapter of First Corinthians.

After years of reading her favorite passages, Thurman finally mustered the temerity to ask his grandmother about her choice of scripture. He wanted to know especially why she shunned anything written by the great apostle Paul. She recounted how, during the days of slavery, her master refused to let the Negro preacher preach to the slaves and always insisted upon a handpicked white preacher, who invariably chose something from Paul, the favorite being "Slaves, be obedient to your masters . . . , as unto Christ." Thurman's grandmother described how the preacher would go on to show how slavery was God's will and to admonish that if they were good and happy slaves, God would bless them. Thurman's grandmother promised the good Lord that if she ever learned to read and if freedom ever came, she would not read that part of the Bible. Thurman's grandmother never learned to read, and that was, I suppose, a sad thing. But she remained a wise woman who knew that you can't trust everything in a book. There's book learning and there's soul learning.

Illiteracy proved to be a blessing to Thurman's grandmother and thousands of others like her who never learned to read the Bible. She was free to hear, remember, and to reread (or have reread to her), as much as she wanted, whatever portions of the Bible suited her. Unencumbered by debates about texts, translations, doctrines, and "Yes, but what does the Bible say?" Thurman's grandmother didn't have to ignore her experiences or suppress her own good senses in order to experience the God of the Bible. She knew good theology when she heard it, and she knew a good God when she met one. In fact, the story of Thurman's grandmother is a lesson in what it means to read, to read sacred texts or secular texts. It is an act that involves both the heart and the mind, an opening up of ourselves to new experiences so that we might be enlarged and might be able to transcend the narrowness of our present life. But that enlarging and transcending do not come about as a result of belittling the world of the reader. Enlarging and transcending happen as the reader acquires the language for and the courage to experiment with new ways of living through the stories told in books.

Reading was akin to an act of worship in the world in which I grew up. It kept us open to the opportunity for inner renewal. It involved more than just calling out words, as my mother was wont to remind me when, as a child sitting in the corner of the kitchen while she cooked dinner, I wanted to hurry through reading my primer in order to get outdoors to join in play with the other children in the neighborhood. Her constant interruptions as I read—"What did you say? Read that to me again" "Is that right?" "What do you think about that Billy Goat?"—were meant to teach me that reading was an encounter, a conversation, between text and reader. Whether reading takes the form of actually calling out the words in a book for ourselves or involves someone else reading its contents for us, the point is that a book is a great book when the characters make us care enough about them to let them live, love, and hate on in our head long after their final epitaph on the page.

Like Thurman's grandmother's, my earliest exposure to the Bible was to an oral experience, more accurately an oral performance. Surrounded as I was as a child by a family full of relatives with inflammable opinions, who took a Friday night game of cards or a Sunday afternoon family dinner as an opportunity to opine heatedly into the wee hours about everything from Lyndon B. Johnson and the blue laws to the moral virtue of moonshine over pot and the best route to take to get to Sparta, Georgia, I was never without the knowledge I needed about the contents of the Bible. The thought of sitting down and reading the Bible would never have occurred to me when I was a child. That would have been like sitting down to read the phone book. And when I would sit down to read it years later, in bits and spurts, of course, I would do so *because* I knew all I needed to know about God, love, and miracles, and not because I was woefully ignorant of such matters and needed to know what the Bible said about these things.

Great books need great readers, someone once said. And great readers make great interpreters, great critics, and great storytellers themselves. Life serves as a great interpreter, helping us, as it did Thurman's grandmother, sift through the junk for the treasures of words, stories, and texts. Great interpreters are not those who have found the one meaning of a text but those who inspire others to voice their own response to the same text. Sometimes if you're a little short on experiences, or short on the necessary experience—as one would expect me to have been as a teenager, just starting out to actually read the Bible—then it helps to have the talents and services of great interpreters, storytellers, preachers, Sunday school teachers, and griots who stir your appetite and your imagination for reading great, though mysterious, books.

My appetite for reading and studying the Bible came along just about the time I was a teenager, when I started taking reading seriously, and it was awakened in a setting that augured the work I'd embark on as my life's journey.

Every Sunday morning, as Sunday school secretary (and thus privy to the deliberations of the adult Bible class), I watched and listened with rapt attention as Elder Briley and Deacon Foxworth openly, publicly, sometimes heatedly railed at each other about the meaning of the morning's Sunday school lesson. The thirty or so adults (and I, the only teenager) who regularly attended the class were mindful to get to Sunday school on time in order to get the best seats, so that we could watch with rapt attention as the pastor and deacon exchanged rhetorical punches about the "true" meaning of the story of creation or the flood; or why only Noah's family was saved; or why God accepted Abel's offering; or how come the Canaanites, Amalekites, and Moabites were destroyed; or how it was possible for Jonah to survive in the belly of a whale; or who was the third person in the fire with the three Hebrew boys (God, Jesus, or the Holy Ghost); or how virgins become pregnant; or how Jesus managed to be both God's son and God's self at the same time; or how many Johns there were in the New Testament; or why it is more likely that the rapture will take place in the day rather than the night. Church school would sometime extend into Sunday worship as the pastor and deacon railed against each other intensely, feverishly, though respectfully, as religious men with no athletic outlet usually do. Each of us sat glued to our spots around the table with our Bibles open, pencils never too far though rarely called upon, listening and reliving the stories through the readings of each man, thumbing through the story in question to follow the argument, but too enthralled by the debate to read for ourselves.

It was a decidedly male sport, to be sure, with all the grandstanding and pontificating that went on; nevertheless, there in the adult Sunday school class in a storefront Pentecostal church I fell in love with the Bible. There also, I learned that interpretation required not merely sharp intellectual reasoning; it also required well-honed rhetorical talents. With little more than a high school education between the two of them, the two men taught me what they knew best, namely, the sacred art of reading stories. They were unlearned about the finer points of interpretation, the science of recovery and reconstructing, and the textuality of stories. But they were masterful about getting their audiences to lean forward and listen to stories, to see themselves in the story, and to care about the story behind the story.

The decision as to which man had succeeded in winning

over the majority of the class to his thinking—which could be calibrated by the roar of our "Amen" and "That's Right!"—depended as much upon each man's oratorical skills as upon his reasoning skills. And what he could not defend by appeal to the manifest letter of the written text (which was usually not much anyway), each man was fully expected to invent. He was to appeal to what, for the moment only, he could see in his mind's eye. The objective, of course, was to persuade the audience to see what he could see. That entailed making the stories come alive; the characters had to walk and talk in ways that were familiar to us, weep over and laugh about things that struck a chord in us. Whatever the scripture's deeper meaning was, whatever God was trying to say or do, had to be humanizing, if not humane. That meant some*body* or some*thing* ought to be changed if God had any part to the story.

Sunday school class, then, not the halls of academia, taught me everything I ever needed to know about imagination and storytelling. Two colored men, unlearned as they were, but who nevertheless walked with God, were the first to model for me study and reading as acts of worship to God. As wild as the interpretations got at times (like the one about Mary being spared labor pains and Jesus being born supernaturally so as to spare him the bloody experience of coming into the world from "down there"), we enjoyed the sheer enjoyment of it all, the telling and retelling of stories. With reverence on some occasions and with tears on other occasions, but often with great laughter, we listened and learned what each man had to say based on his reading of scripture. Reinforced in my Sunday school class were all my mother's lessons about study and reading as acts of worship. Both required considerable leaps of the imagination, which was precisely where God dwelled, just beyond the realm of reason but fully within the grasp of the human heart.

Every week I had the opportunity to witness a handful of common, mostly illiterate black women and men who were janitors, cooks, beauticians, porters, and schoolteachers during the week but, come Sunday, were transformed by God into scholars, lawyers, scribes, philosophers, and storytellers—all of them children of ex-slaves in search of a God they could trust. In masterful strokes of the imagination, crafting his arguments to the sensibilities of his listeners, bringing to life the subliminal human drama at the surface of stories, appealing to the morning's scripture to digress and expound by analogy to contemporary events, each man would bring his argument to a close by turning to his audience with the words, "Do you see what I'm saying?"

To this day, I still believe that the best compliment to a book or a sermon is, "I see what you mean."

Revival

I said I wasn't going to tell nobody, but I just couldn't keep it to myself.

NEGRO GOSPEL SONG

It is a common scene from my evangelical past. The evangelist has finished preaching and people in the congregation sit on the edge of their pews waiting, tense with anticipation. The evangelist has preached about salvation, sanctification, predestination, or something on that order. It's the fourth night of a five-night church revival, and the young, charismatic evangelist from out of town has mesmerized everyone all week long with his mellifluous singing. Tonight he sings the famous hymn "Just as I Am." It's now time for him to switch his talents from being an evangelist to being a prophet. A revivalist isn't fit to be followed if his word isn't backed up with signs and wonders. He must either heal someone or predict someone's future, or both. That's the tradition of these events. Every night after his sermon, the evangelist stands quietly at the front of the church looking contemplatively, after which his eyes fall on someone in the congregation and he beckons that person up to the front, where he stands. This is the highlight of the service. Time for the word to move from the universal to the particular.

I am sitting in the church with the less than one hundred people who have come out to witness this event. Like everyone else, I try to avoid the evangelist's gaze, not wishing to seem as though I'm begging for a blessing.

"You. Yes, you. The young girl in the green checkered blouse. Yes, you."

I sit frozen in my seat, pretending he isn't pointing to me. But I know he is. I don't bother to look down at the blouse I'm wearing. I fell in love with its lovely green checks the moment I saw it at the department store. After a few seconds of everyone in the church looking around to see exactly who the evangelist is talking about, all eyes fall on my blouse and travel up to my face. I point to myself and raise my eyebrows just to be sure.

"Yes, you. Come here. The Lord has a word for your life."

"Lord, no," I complain as I peel myself slowly from my pew and make my way up to the front of the church, where the young evangelist waits. Every eye in the small congregation is on me. Tambourines are quieted. The organist has stopped playing. I'm nervous. I wonder how I look from the back. My hair. My shoes. One sock won't stay up. I wonder about the zipper on the back of my skirt. Is it straight? I want to reach for it and check. But I decide against it. I'm embarrassed by the attention. I hear my stepmother somewhere in the back of the church shout, "Praise the Lord. Hallelujah. That's my child." Soon I'm standing eyeball to eyeball with the man at the front of the church.

"What's your name, daughter?"

"Renita."

"Renita, how old are you?"

"Seventeen."

"Renita, do you love Jesus?"

"Yes sir."

"Young lady, do you believe that the Lord can speak to you?"

"Yes sir."

His eyes are earnest and warm and stare straight at me. Despite my shyness I try earnestly to look him straight in his eyes. He is certainly more handsome close up than five pews away. My eyes blink uncontrollably and I can't do a thing about it. He lifts one arm up to put a hand on my shoulder, and the smell of cologne mixed with his sweat wafts into my nostril. A Bible is in his other hand.

This is a special moment in every believer's life. Everyone else in the congregation would die to trade places with me at that moment. To be touched by the man of God. To be the sole object of his prophetic gaze. To know that the Lord is speaking to you through the prophet. What will he say? Will he condemn you for some secret or not-so-secret sin that stands between your soul and the Savior? Or will he commend you? If I were an adult, say, the age of my stepmother, he'd probably praise me for my years of faithfulness, honesty, hard work, and sacrifice, and then conclude promising that a reward was imminent, preferably in the form of material prosperity. Three months of bills paid without fail is cause to make the working class jump up and shout uncontrollably. But I'm only seventeen. And I don't have any bills. The prophet, instead, speaks vaguely and nebulously about God seeing my youth, commending my innocence and my commitment in coming out every night for revival despite there being school in the morning. For my devotion, God is going to use me in the future to do great works for him, he promises, or something along that line.

Come to think about it, evangelists were always beckoning me to come up front to stand with them. They were always laying their hands on my head, just as you see on television, or placing a hand on my forehead or on my shoulder as prelude to a show of their prophetic powers. Those called to the front were supposed to fall on the floor when the prophet laid his hand on them, as a result of the power of the prophet's anointing. But I never fell down. I stood, I listened attentively, and I returned to my seat as sober as I had left it. This bothered some of the evangelists. At first I thought something was wrong with me because I didn't fall. But greater was my fear of what God might do if I faked the fall than was my fear of God's wrath at my not falling. Besides, I was always afraid that I might bump my head and hurt myself, or that my dress might fly up when I fell, as some others' did, and then I'd be hurt and humiliated.

I always obeyed and rose from my seat when evangelists called me to the front, because I believed God spoke through evangelists—not always, but enough times to warrant, if you're around one, getting up and going to check out what he or she has to say. And even when I had my own doubts about whether certain ones could be trusted, I got up anyway when they called me out, out of politeness. I was certain that some evangelists had the gift, that they could discern my lustful appetites, the fact that I cursed at school around my friends, that I cut classes sometimes and hung out with friends, that I'd swiped ice cream bars and bags of candy from corner stores. With all the guilt I carried around inside, I was sure that sooner or later one of them would announce to the whole church that he could see straight through me to my wicked heart. But none of them ever did. If they ever saw the truth, they never told my secrets. I was convinced that I was being called out because God was warning me to straighten up. Regardless, I could never allow myself to fall.

Of the scores of evangelists who came through my church, only one of them ever said anything to me worth remembering. And even now I'm not sure whether what I think he said is what he actually said or is only what my seventeen-year-old lonely heart wished he'd said. He was the sincerest of all of them—or that was my impression of him. He was also the cutest. "Young lady, where you are at this moment is not where you will be next year," he looked in my eyes and said.

That's it. That's all I remember. Of course, I didn't need a prophet to tell me the obvious. What would make me carry this sentence around in my head all these years? It's certainly not because a visiting evangelist spoke these words to me, although I will always be grateful for what he said, or think he said. I'm grateful because, of all the things he could have said to enhance his image as a prophet, he didn't say any of those things. He said something so obvious, so generic, so banal, so ordinary that it has always stuck out in my mind. I heard God.

He didn't say, *"who* you are at this moment," but, *"where* you are at this moment." The difference got my attention. I'm ashamed to admit that I'm still basically the same bashful, moody, frightened, curious, stubborn, boy-crazed girl who is too proud to make a spectacle of herself even for God that I was at seventeen years of age. That basic self, to my disgrace, has not changed. I'm still bashful about getting up in front of people, but now as a minister and university professor I don't have a choice. I remain moody, frightened, curious, and a dozen other things, too many to enumerate here. Nevertheless, the self adapts, even if it doesn't change. I am the same self, but he was right that I'm no longer at the same emotional, intellectual, and spiritual level I was more than twenty years ago. I didn't crumble to the floor when he put his hand on me, although a side of me wanted to. Instead, I stumbled back to my pew and slumped down in my seat and stared at nothing in particular for the rest of the evening. I can't say that I understood fully what the young evangelist meant at the time. At the time, I didn't, in fact. But in time I would.

We learn to grow and to adapt in light of changing circumstances and changing seasons; we stumble upon doors we didn't know were there; we grope for light we barely make out; and some*where* in the process of it all, some*where* between laughing and crying, as we look back at all the *where*s our stubborn, frightened self has been, we make out some meaning and direction to our life, not of our own making but of someone else's making, someone more intelligent, yes, but also someone with an infinitely better sense of humor than we have.

Whenever someone tries to talk to me about the difficulty of recognizing the voice or presence of God, my mind goes back to the revivals I attended as a girl. I never mention my experiences with the many fake but also the few honest evangelists that came through town. I wouldn't know where to begin to talk about all the confession, laughter, tears, and love that are wrapped up in all of those years. There's no way I can make anyone understand that just beneath the surface of all the drama, the naiveté, and the farce, God was at work—not just in my life, I suppose, but in the other lives that were touched by those revivals as well.

Of course, education tends to make us look back at our conservative, working-class origins with contempt. In order to gain acceptance into the upper classes, in order to buy into academia, in order to move around in a class of educated clergy, for the sake of upward mobility, we must denigrate the people, the experiences, and all the memories that shaped us. If we're not careful, education can make us hate and scoff at our past. With thirty years of experience and education under my belt, numerous academic publications to my credit, new-found middle-class sensibilities, an acquired taste for recognition among my peers, I'm supposed to look back and laugh at all those nights I spent in church revival while I was a teenager. How stupid could I have been back then? What a bunch of ignoramuses all of us in the church were, to be under the spell of one jackleg, uneducated, cunning evangelist after another who did nothing more than tap into our working-class fears, exploit our weaknesses, and tell us things we wanted to hear. In exchange for their placebos, we flocked to the altar at night and laid at their feet our rent money, our grocery money, children's lunch money, and the carfare we had to get to work. What a sight! How sad. How pitiful. And what do any of us have to show for all that belief? A heart full of hope which keeps me tiptoeing to the altar.

I Too Have a Dream

The subject of the dream is the dreamer.

TONI MORRISON

The dreams that are so absurd that they make me bolt up in the bed in the middle of the night and keep me tossing and turning until dawn are the first ones to get my attention. Gotta be God. Take the dream (when I've had too much coffee) of me standing in the pulpit preaching in my slip. It doesn't take a rocket scientist to figure out what fear lies beneath that scandal. What are you saying, God? How much more naked and vulnerable do you expect me to be in the pulpit? I ask in a fit of sleeplessness. Then there are the dreams that wake me up with their terror. Running, hiding, and always trying to get away from God-knows-what-and-who is one I dream at least once a month. After forty-something years I still haven't been able to make out the face of the one chasing me. But one thing is constant: he is persistent—and I'm always one step away from being caught.

Some dreams are forgotten the moment we awake. But the ones we remember, whether laughing or trembling, are the ones worth examining. Sometimes in our dreams are kernels of truth, pinches of revelation, whispers of God's voice.

One dream recurs every year. I call it my "visitation" dream. Coming as it does (at least in my mind) from somewhere beyond the realm of mere dreams, somewhere between reality and the unconscious, I discern that more is going on in my subconscious than my intellect can fathom. The first visitation dream occurred when I was a teenager, and it occurred more frequently in my twenties and thirties, but its appearances have decreased over the last nine years. After "visiting" me often when I was young, its "visits" are down to once a year now. The first one occurred when I was seventeen and I'd only had the bedroom to myself for a short while (my stepsister Brenda had moved away only a few months earlier). I remember turning over in my bed in the middle of the night and noticing the outline of two people sitting on the twin bed on the other side of the room, where Brenda once slept. I couldn't make out their faces because the room was too dark. I kept focusing, but try as I might, nothing was clear but their silhouettes. Whether they were male or female presences I can't say for sure now. All I recall is that both were sitting on the bed thumbing through a book. The sound of pages turning filled the bedroom. The two people spoke to each other in whispers that were barely audible over the turning pages. After about two, three, maybe four minutes, they got up and left the room. Just like that. They came and they went without so much as looking at me, but communicated with me the whole time. I remember running down the stairs and waking up my stepmother, who was the most God-fearing and spiritual woman I knew at the time. It didn't hurt that she kept a dream book next to her bed.

My stepmother (God bless her) woke up and joined me in the kitchen for some juice and permitted me to tell her as much as I could recall about the strange visitation. She heard me out, poured us both some juice, and without appearing the least bit surprised or flabbergasted by the dream, assured me that the people in my dream were probably angels coming to tell me something. What they were trying to tell me, she didn't seem to know, or I can't remember what she said, except that they were probably sent to alert me that books, words, and surely the Bible were going to figure prominently in my future.

The visitation dreams have continued with me over the years. My visitors have inched closer since their first appearance. Increasingly they're less *out there,* across the room, and more right upon me, nearer, sitting on the foot of the bed with me, saying little at all, just content to be near me. I read recently that 43 percent of Americans say that they have had some sort of mystical experience in the past few years but have not been able to talk about it with people. That is supposed to comfort me. At least I know I'm not alone in my experiences. But knowing those figures, I realize that I am not special, either. I never feel any danger when my visitors are present, only a jostling and moving around to get my attention. We've never exchanged words, even though, each time, I tell myself to relax and say something. But nothing comes to mind. What do you say to angelic visitors? I'm convinced that the visitors are from the beyond, but who they are and what they want to tell me remain unclear. For now I am content to be able to know when they're present.

Wherever dreams come from, and I don't pretend to know where that is, it's a place within each of us, down within our souls, a place that won't take *no, shut up, not now, you again?* for an answer. It's a place that demands our attention and resolves to get it, whether with laughter or with terror. It's a place within which insists that we remember the lives we have lived, says Frederic Beuchner. It calls upon us to remember memories, remember emotions, remember moments, remember things we've tried furiously to avoid or to forget. Dreams beckon us into a still room within us where it is safe to remember where our journeys have brought us. It is safe because it's a place where we can face our fears, anger, and dread and see them for what they were and are: feelings that needn't last forever. It is safe because no one has access to that room, save you and God. And there in that room filled with our greatest anxieties, God meets us and beckons, "Come, it is time to be healed."

Each time a dream has enough current in it to awaken us, God is speaking to us through some chamber within us, beckoning us to come in. It's time. It's time to remember. It's time to lighten up. It's time to sort through. It's time to heal. It's time to let go. It's time to learn how to laugh at ourselves.

The Welcome Table

The greatest gift is not being afraid to question.

RUBY DEE

After being raised, during my adolescent years, in the Pentecostal church, when I went away to college in the early seventies and joined a Methodist church in the Boston area that was popular among college students, I found myself mourning the loss of certain staple elements from my conservative charismatic-church upbringing. Even though my new church family, well known for both its spirited worship and socially progressive ministries in the community, better suited my newly acquired Brahmin tastes, I missed, nevertheless, the close-knit, insular, partisan world of Pentecostalism and the sense of moral superiority bred among Pentecostalists, believing as they do that they are the elect. When I switched from being a Pentecostal and became a Methodist, I gave up belonging to a tradition that made me feel I had a moral and spiritual edge over others.

After more than twelve years in ministry in the Methodist church, I jumped the marriage broom with, of all things, a Baptist minister and found myself regularly attending his small Baptist church in Nashville and singing with him from the same hymnal. I felt rudderless in the free-church tradition of Baptist worship services and started longing for a bit of the liturgical and ceremonial graces I'd come to expect in Methodist worship. Above all, I missed the sublime music of Methodist hymnody and the stately cadences of collects taken straight out of the Book of Common Prayer—*"It is very meet, right, and our bounden duty, that we should at all times, and in all places, give thanks unto thee, O Lord, Almighty, Everlasting God."*

Ah yes. I missed worshiping with Methodists, and I resented giving up the rich cadences of that tradition and the psychological satisfaction it gave me. I resisted joining the Baptist church—and I quickly remind my husband of this point when I have to put distance between me and some of the lamebrain, fundamentalist, parochial pronouncements made by certain Baptist sects. Marrying a Baptist, as I have, however, makes me feel guilty and personally liable for every misguided religious edict issued by the denomination.

Let's face it: there's nothing exotic about being a Methodist minister and ex-Pentecostal who is now married to a Baptist preacher. Nothing exotic about it at all. No wonder I haven't heard a word from God. What do Pentecostals, Methodists, or Baptists know about the deeper, more subtle mysteries of the spiritual journey? Ask any Protestant and she'll tell you that if you want to hear what God has to say, why, read the Bible. That's why it's called the word of God. Of course, my friends in the so-called high Christian churches argue that as an ex-Pentecostal, now Methodist, who is married to a Baptist, I'm at a distinct disadvantage spiritually. I lack the scaffolding for building up my spiritual life. Look at what I've been missing in these traditions. No incense. No chants. No saints. No beads. No icons. No heroes dressed up in baroque headgear and ostentatious robes. And worst of all, no liturgy to speak of. In short, no mystery. Absolutely nothing to inspire awe or incredulity. Low church, free church, whatever—any tradition that tries to sell God as right here, visible, on the verge of appearing any minute right before your very eyes without any genuflecting on our part is an inferior church. Everyone knows that if you really want to get the inside scoop on God and discover the secrets of prayer, you must read the Catholics. Now, there's the way to go. They have more than a millennium head start over Baptists, Methodists, and Pentecostals on such matters. If you insist that the pope is wrong about abortion, women's ordination, and a host of other things, there's always the Episcopal church, the great-aunt of the Methodist Episcopal church. They have the best of both worlds: they have the liturgical trappings of the Catholic church, so that when you leave their services you depart feeling as though you'd just been part of something heady, exotic, and wondrous. But they spare you the moral pronouncements and don't ask anything of you, so you can go on doing whatever suits you and not have to bother with feeling guilty about anything.

I don't know what to expect anymore. Stripped of the social and moral edge I once enjoyed when I was a puffed-up

Pentecostal and when I was a proud Methodist, and now adrift in a sea of spiritual apathy and inner silence, I don't know what to expect anymore from the trove of traditions I have to choose from. I'm afraid to put too much trust in denominational traditions, even though I am convinced that I am not one to declare my independence from institutional religion and to strike out on some New Age self-induced state of contemplation. I need and enjoy the thorns and thistles of institutional religion as it helps me to sharpen, hammer out, sound out, and routinize my beliefs. Institutional religion has both blessed me and injured me by handing me some expectations about God that I can test out. Thankfully, God confirmed some of those expectations. Thankfully, God ignored a great many of those expectations. But it was both in confirming a few and in ignoring a great many other of my expectations that God offered me a chance for inner discovery and growth. I felt safe and smug in my tradition when God confirmed my expectations, and I was forced to pause and reexamine my motives and prejudices when God has not responded to me in ways I expected. It is because (and not simply despite the fact that) I risked becoming attached to Pentecostal, Methodist, and Baptist traditions, I believe, that I learned the freedom of faith, hope, and love.

I've caught myself driving down a street lost in my own thoughts and pausing for a moment to look through the rearview mirror, wondering how I managed to drive through one traffic light and two stop signs without remembering either. Similarly, I catch myself at times kneeling on Sundays and not remembering when and how in the world I managed to get out of bed, dress myself, come to the church, and get through three-fifths of the service without thinking about it. But I'm grateful to have a place, some place, any place, regardless of tradition, where I can go intuitively, without thinking, for no other reason than that its doors are open and there is room for one more, and I'm thankful for a raggedy community of people who wait there to help me out of my coat and escort me to a seat where I may sit, think, sing, and kneel until it comes back to me what is so sacred about sitting, thinking, singing, and kneeling with others.

The Tap of an Angel

Oh, oh, oh, oh, somebody touched me. And it must have been the hand of the Lord.

NEGRO SPIRITUAL

At the close of an otherwise forgettable semester in a class on New Testament theology, the professor, a remarkably uninspiring sort who never spoke above a whisper and seemed utterly incapable of answering a question without a question—which might make for a provocative pedagogical style if, as a student, you didn't have to worry about grades and trying to pass core courses—this professor, who until the end of that semester was never my favorite professor because he never looked us straight in the face but went around with his eyes cast to the ground, always looking as though he was lost in thinking about thinking, said something the last day of class that came as close to a benediction as ever I've been able to recognize. Removing his glasses and in characteristic fashion wiping them with the lapel of his tweed jacket, he said in a whisper to a class of students anxious to be dismissed so we might get a head start on the holiday travelers leaving Princeton for the Christmas break: "And now go out and preach with a bad conscience, knowing that for everything you choose to say in the pulpit, there was something you chose not to say, could have said, but for your own desperate reasons chose to ignore. Preach your best, my friends, and then be quick to sit down forever looking over your shoulder at any moment for the disapproving tap of an angel."

I never recovered from my professor's benediction. It leaves me slightly choked up at the end of sermons. It is somewhere stirring in my heart whenever I dismiss a class at the end of the semester, ashamed of all the things that didn't take place that semester or couldn't be done in a semester, and all the things, for whatever reasons, that weren't or couldn't be grasped.

Strange how people hear things differently. My study partner and best friend in graduate school heard the same words of our fumbling New Testament professor as a curse. She felt paralyzed. They are the kind of words, she argued, that seep into your consciousness and nip away at your professional confidence, causing you to second-guess yourself, making it difficult for you to decide upon what to say, robbing you of the ability to take pride in your work, leaving you stuttering in sermons and lessons. But that's not what I heard. I thought I heard an angel. Relieved of the pressure to be perfect, of having to get it just right, I was freed to tell a story about flawed people grappling to find the words to tell the story of a God they think they saw and think they heard on some mountain, in some cave, by some seashore, at some supper table. The benediction by an otherwise forgettable teacher at the close of an unspectacular semester of study freed me to preach and teach in ways that might inspire others, including myself, to pray. My task as a believer is not to inspire those who come out to hear me to believe, but to help open up a space in each of them so that belief, if it ever comes, may have someplace to take root and grow.

Holy Ground

Take off your shoes, for the ground you are standing on is holy ground.

EXODUS 3:5

It is Sunday morning, a few minutes before eleven o'clock, and I am on my way as a seminarian to preach at an African Methodist Episcopal church in a small town in central New Jersey. I wish I could say that the invitation to preach was the initiative of the pastor of the church, that he extended it to me as one colleague to another. But I cannot say this. Today is Women's Day at this small African Methodist Episcopal church, and I have been summoned to bring the morning message because I'm one of a handful of woman preachers in this part of the state and because, living as I do only two towns over in Princeton, I'm the closest to the church. As the single largest fund-raising event in many black churches, Women's Day has forced the Methodist pastor to acquiesce to the pressure the female members have exerted on him to invite a lady preacher. It's perhaps the only day in the church year when women in this small church have a say in the way things go. My task is twofold: encourage the women to continue their exemplary work of cooking, praying, visiting the sick, financially supporting the church; and say nothing about the imbalance of power between women and men in the church. It's only the fifth sermon I've preached in my life, and already I've made enemies in central Jersey. The week before, a pastor escorted me out of his pulpit, informing me that the women had made a mistake in inviting me; he didn't allow women in his pulpit.

I arrive at this church this morning filled with apprehension. I don't know what to expect. Will it be a cordial, or a cool, reception? Will I be permitted to preach, and if I am, will I have to preach from a lectern on the floor of the church, or be allowed to join the pastor in the pulpit? What will I do if these people react to me as those in another church, fifty miles down the road, did last month, with stony silence? I think, There's still time to turn around and go home. Already my stomach is doing somersaults as the time draws near.

As usual, I am running a little late. Instead of arriving at 10:30 A.M. as I promised, I am reaching in the backseat of my car for my Bible at 10:50 A.M. and praying that I did not forget to bring my long slip to wear under my long white robe. I make my way up the steep steps to the church, mindful to greet parishioners dashing in the same direction ("Good Morning," "Praise the Lord"). As I climb the steps my mind flashes back to eighteenth- and nineteenth-century colored women preachers who were barred from preaching in established black pulpits. Women like Jarena Lee, Amanda Berry Smith, and Maria Stewart were denied ordination and had to content themselves with the labels of "exhorter," "evangelist," and "mighty fine speaker," when their gifts of oratory frequently exceeded those of the men who refused them the pulpit. I think of Jarena Lee and Amanda Berry Smith, both nineteenth-century women who satisfied themselves with traveling thousands of miles to exhort and testify and lead prayer meetings. Jarena Lee, born in Cape May, New Jersey, in 1783, described herself in her memoirs as "the first female preacher of the First African Methodist Episcopal Church." The founder of the denomination and its first bishop, Richard Allen, endorsed Lee's desire to preach but staunchly refused to ordain her. Amanda Berry Smith, who started out as a washerwoman, had to wait until her husband died before she could be free, in 1878, to travel and preach, and then, of course, without benefit of ordination. Her preaching, coupled with her immense talents as a singer, secured her mission assignments as far away as England, India, and Liberia. As for Jarena Lee, just for an invitation to come and pray, Lee would have had to start out Saturday morning in a buggy from Cape May or, if need be, on foot to arrive on time to this central Jersey church. Driving as I do, more than a century later, a midsize Chevrolet, I should be able to arrive earlier for these services, but I don't because I want to be spared the looks and stares.

An usher is waiting for me at the door to the church, dressed in an impeccably white uniform with matching shoes and gloves. She doesn't try to hide her disapproval. She takes a hard look at me and beckons me to follow her to the back of the church, where the pastor's study is located. We make our way through a throng of women greeting one another with kisses and pinning corsages to one another's dresses, and grandmothers guiding little ones to the water fountain and rest room for the last time before service begins. Stolen glances follow me as I make my way with the usher to the back of the church. From the corners of my eyes I notice fingers pointing in my direction. Before I turn the final corner to the pastor's study, an anxious whisper from the choir room reaches my shoulder: "Is that the lady preacher?"

"It seems so," a less anxious voice answers.

"Come, Jesus."

> We're marching to Zion,
> Beautiful, beautiful Zion;
> We're marching upwards to Zion,
> That beautiful city of God.

The female choir prepares to march into the sanctuary. Across the church, women, men, and children stand to join the choir in thanking God for another week's journey. Old women in stockings rolled up to their thighs, with hats that resemble crowns of petals, help one another to their feet. Old men blow their noses with starched white handkerchiefs. Others clasp children with one hand and wave the other in gratitude. I stand alone in the pulpit waiting for the choir and other liturgists to join me. All eyes are in my direction, but not on me. They are gazing up at the gilded cross just above my head. It is much too ornate to make one think of death; still, it is austere enough to make one think of unrelenting pain. The choir marches in. The musician closes her eyes. And the whole congregation rocks back and forth to a pulse we know well.

> I was glad when they said unto me,
> "Let us go into the house
> of the Lord."

The call to worship is drawn from one of the psalms. The words serve to remind us that we are *here* and not elsewhere, reassuring us that it's safe to let go, that we can trust our hearts to have led us to the right place. The schoolteacher is reminded that she is the sister of the domestic worker, the doctor's wife holds the hand of the welfare mother, the civil servant shares a pew with the bootlegger. We are the church, a ragged band of miracle workers: ragged because we are often contentious, scared, lazy, undependable, and—in a word—flawed; miracle workers because we've had to take straw and build a cathedral of hope for every generation that crossed our threshold.

Soon an overdressed woman wearing shades of blue makes her way to the front of the church. I recognize her by her smile. She is, no doubt, the church clerk. For years her job has been to read the church announcements. A waitress in a Shoney's restaurant, a maid in a hotel, a clerk in a toll booth, she toils much of the week in an environment where no one knows or cares to know her name. But on Sunday mornings she glows in her responsibility as the church's press secretary. I look at her and wonder how many *other* women, professional women—lawyers, speechwriters, journalists, professors like myself—acquired their earliest speaking skills in their mother's church. How many of us learned our first lessons in women's politics in the Ladies' Mission Circle? Many important lessons are passed along here. We learn what it means to hold fast to visions others cannot see. The woman in blue reminds the congregation about the benefit next Sunday to raise money for one of the high school graduates who is in dire need of money for books as he heads off for his first semester of college in a few weeks. Then there's the clothes drive for the family whose home was gutted by fire.

I listen to the endless list of tasks taken up by the church, close my eyes, and wonder, Where are all the militants of an earlier era who shook their fists at the church and resolved to shoot their way into the Promised Land? From what I can tell, the militants traded their guns for Volvos. And the ladies of Stewardess Board No. 3 and the Women's Usher Board are left once again to plough the fields of the people's sorrow.

The altar is now open for those of you who wish to come and kneel before the mercy seat.

The organist plays softly "Sweet Hour of Prayer." Lines of people, some well dressed and some shabbily clothed, gather from all corners of the church to come to the altar. Each waits his or her turn to kneel around the plain wooden rail. Those unable to kneel stand and bow their heads. Hope is not in the kneeling but in the telling. Grandmothers and young mothers, grandfathers and uncles wait their turn to tell Jesus all about addicted sons who steal from them, teenage granddaughters pregnant for the third time, employers who humiliate them, and arthritis that cripples the knees. "Lord, see us as we travel through this low land of sorrow" is how the older gentleman in the front pew put it in the corporate prayer. Some bow their heads, while others look up toward the ceiling. Some weep openly, while others stare straight ahead without a word. Each is transfixed in prayer, filled with the need to draw closer to God's presence. Most have given up praying for solutions. Strength is miracle enough. The sight of one's mother or father hunched over a simple wooden rail with their heads bowed might embarrass an adult child. Old-fashioned. Counterrevolutionary. Futile. Undignified. But Ruth Dead's question to her insolent son Macon Dead Jr. in the novel *Song of Solomon,* seems appropriate: "What harm did I do you on my knees?"

> I believe in God, the Father Almighty,
> Maker of heaven and earth . . .
> I believe in the Holy Ghost, the holy Catholic Church . . .

Believing is not the hard part; waiting is. Waiting on God. Trusting the Holy Ghost. Since there's no way to rush, either, we have had to take some things in our own hands, such as building our own church. The Catholic church of the Apostles' Creed does not refer to the Roman Catholic church but attests to our belief that the church is essentially, one, universal, and open to all. We are a segregated church at this moment, but we didn't start out that way. In 1787 a handful of black Methodists, many of whom were members of a mutual aid association made up of Philadelphia's free black population known as the Free African Society, walked out of Saint George's Church in Philadelphia after a scuffle broke out between black worshipers and white trustees of the church, who interrupted the Africans as they were praying and demanded that they get up from their knees and move to the segregated part of the sanctuary reserved for blacks. The freedmen's decision to leave behind decades of the "unkind treatment of their white brethren" at Saint George's Methodist Episcopal Church and to found their own separate worship society, the African Methodist Episcopal church, gave rise to a black separatist worship movement throughout post-Revolutionary America and gave free Africans all over the courage to break away from their white Protestant benefactors and create for themselves a safe place to worship, away from the scrutinizing eyes of white people.

Segregated worship was a sad necessity then, and it is now. But those worshiping here this morning have come to accept sadness as a fact of life.

Come by here, dear Lord, come by here. O Lord, come by here.

A little brown girl who reminds me of myself at that age waits her turn at the altar. Her shiny eyes stare intently up at me in the pulpit. Hers are eyes a thousand years old, full of awe and hope. When she is old she will remember this day and me, the lady preacher, as I remember women who came before me. There was Sister Lottie Noble, who rose from her pew every Sunday and sang, "God is a good God, yes he is," before launching into some testimony about God's mercy and grace, and Miss Nancy, my stepmother, who didn't know how to worship without weeping. Since we can not speak or touch, I blow a kiss in the little brown girl's direction. I want to assure her that I know what little girls pray for: fighting parents, bullies at school, bedridden grandmothers, and blu*est* eyes. Someone behind her nudges her toward an empty space at the altar.

I close my eyes and pray for the task at hand. I pray that the sermon I have spent days thinking about will suit this congregation. I pray that it is helpful, illuminating, and inspiring. I pray that it makes a difference that I came two towns over to speak to this church today.

In the background of my prayer I hear a very familiar story:

This morning we are very blessed to have as our preacher the Reverend Renita Weems, who is a woman well equipped and called by the Lord . . .

I cast my eyes to the floor, embarrassed by my own testimony: a bachelor's degree from a New England women's college, graduate study at Princeton, and publications to my credit. The woman talks glowingly about the "sacrifices" I made for ministry, abandoning a career with a major brokerage firm on Wall Street (I was actually on my way to being fired), giving up membership in the Black Panther Party (I volunteered at a friend's urging to help the organization serve breakfast to hungry children for three weekends in a row). I don't dare look up at anyone, lest someone see through me to the truth. A résumé is a genre of half-truths, a fictionalized self that never represents the full story, stretched and misinterpreted to enhance the product. No résumé can possibly tell the real story behind my journey into ministry, a story I cannot fully explain myself. I didn't choose ministry so much as ministry chose me. I hope I heard correctly, but I can't always be sure. No dungeons shook, or chains fell; nothing out of the ordinary happened to convince me. I didn't hear a voice as most of my eighteenth- and nineteenth-century predecessors in Methodism, such as Jarena Lee, Richard Allen, Amanda Berry Smith, and Rebecca Cox Jackson, repeatedly claimed. No floodlight illumining my path, just a tiny shaft of light here and there, not enough to blind me but just enough to keep me groping for the switch.

The congregation listens to the half story of my life, nods, and murmurs with awe. They are always proud when one of their young makes it out. They study the tall brown woman with short, cropped hair sitting beneath the cross, and they smile approvingly, grateful. Some look at me and think of their own children—their daughters in San Francisco, New York City, or Atlanta who have abandoned the sanctuary choir for occasional volunteerism, for sorority functions, and for Sunday brunches. They look at me and wonder if there is still hope for their daughters and sons, who have grown more enamored with power than with prayer. This morning I must preach to mothers and fathers who have been praying for as long as I have been alive. I wonder what I can say that they don't already know. And if I do have something helpful to say, why has God waited so long to say it and then done so through such an unlikely vehicle?

My heart beats rapidly and my palms grow moist as the time draws near. It is a frightening thing to be used by God. My stepmother's words fifteen years earlier come back to me as I recall her standing over me with comb in her hands: "Neetie, God got his hands on you and he's got a work for you to do." I was only a teenager then, too young and impatient to imagine the burden of being blessed.

But now . . . well, now the singing has ceased. The church is quiet. All attention is upon me. I stand and open my Bible. I think of the women and men who have stood in this same place over the years—preaching, praying, testifying, singing away misery—and I understand what it is to stand on *holy ground.*

I turn to what would become one of my favorite passages in the Bible (from the second book of Chronicles), open my mouth, and feel my soul kneel slowly before the sacredness of this moment. I do not know that the sermon this Sunday will be one that will haunt me for the rest of my life. I do not know that I will be preaching about a silence, a grappling in the dark, a hoping against hope that, as a woman, a preacher, and a pilgrim I will return to again and again in my spiritual journey.

O our God . . . we do not know what to do.
But our eyes are upon thee.

The Itinerant Journey

The longest journey
Is the journey inwards
Of him who has chosen his destiny.

DAG HAMMARSKJÖLD

With all the pomp and grandiloquence that marks such ceremonies, Bishop Richard Hildebrand of the African Methodist Episcopal Church, along with a retinue of ministers, laid his hands on my head in 1984 and declared over me and some ten others kneeling at the altar waiting to be ordained, "The Lord pour upon thee the Holy Ghost for the office and work of an itinerant elder in the Church of God, now committed unto thee by the imposition of our hands." With these words, and under the weight of their calloused hands, I was being sent out into an itinerant system, of wandering from post to post, from people to people, from charge to charge, from need to need, never staying in one place too long but belonging to a network of believers beyond any one place, a personification of the universal mission of Christianity to "go into all the world." The call to preach, according to the Wesleyan tradition, is a call to be always ready to uproot and travel. It is the apostolic plan, or so argued the founding fathers of Methodism, which has as its focus the universal spread of the gospel.

Ministers in the Methodist tradition are ordained into an itinerancy system that seemed at the time of John Wesley, the founder, and Bishop Francis Asbury, one of the first bishops of the church, ideally suited for reaching the isolated populations that were spread out across the vast eighteenth-century American frontier. Think of the Wesley itinerant system and the image that comes to mind is of the circuit preacher riding his horse from town to town, over fields, through marshes, around forests, across rivers, and through brush arbors. Itinerancy means journeying, and Bishop Hildebrand sent me out on an itinerant journey back in 1984, fully expecting me to go out and find my way on a journey without a map, without an itinerary, in search of a destination yet to be discovered. Normally, someone who just takes off on a journey with no earthly idea where she is going is called a vagabond, a bum, a Gypsy. But I am called Reverend.

Mystics have been hard pressed to come up with a better metaphor to describe the inner life of growing, stretching, climbing, retreating, scrambling, slumping, and soaring that the soul endures than to refer to it as a voyage, a path, a way, a pilgrimage, a journey. And I am hard pressed to characterize the unpredictability and inconstancy of that journey as anything other than itinerant. Itinerancy captures for me the inner journey, the going with no particular destination in view, no itinerary, and no arrival time, living on the road, traveling from circuit to circuit, along a path that twists and curves from morning to evening, across valleys and plains. "Praying and listening for God on the run" is the way one spiritual guide put it to me. It means living every day open, accepting what the journey brings us, relying on nothing but faith in God to get us from one location to the next. It is the hardest thing in the world to get accustomed to: constantly wondering whether you're getting anywhere, never sure if you're where you ought to be, feeling as though you're wandering and circling the same spot again and again.

Being a Protestant makes the itinerant journey especially

unrattling. Bereft of the tradition, the liturgy, the feasts, the reverent spiritual fathers and mothers, the spiritual readings, and the disciplines for spiritual formation that Catholic friends can draw from in their traditions, Protestants are left to muddle through the Bible to find rules of life and daily disciplines to aid them in connecting with God. Luther's argument that grace and the divine were revealed *sola scriptura*—by scripture alone—was in principle a great and salutary reform measure, intended as it was to demythologize ecclesial authority and to make God's word accessible to all. But in his polemic against church structure and traditions, Luther left followers like me scrambling to find our bearings along this pilgrimage from nowhere in particular to (presumably) somewhere ultimately. Although the circuit preacher couldn't be sure from one month to the next where he would be sent by the ruling authorities, he could at least count on there being a trail in the forest left by previous riders and wagon trains as a guide to the next town. As a Protestant I've felt as though I have had to make up my way as I've gone along, traveling oftentimes without a map, having to rely solely on my own wits.

At my ordination, the preacher for the service preached from a scripture that I had never given any thought to before: *"When Pharaoh let the people go, God did not lead them by way of the land of the Philistines, although that was nearer; for God thought, If the people face war, they may change their minds and return to Egypt. So God led the people by the roundabout way of the wilderness toward the Red Sea."* I thought I knew a lot, as a doctoral student in Old Testament studies, about the Exodus story as an archetype of the journey story. But I was completely ignorant of some important details of that story. There was a shortcut to their destination, but God sent the

Hebrew children the winding, indirect way in order to save and protect them from their own fears and insecurities. The ordination preacher reminded us of the often circuitous nature, the roundaboutness, of the spiritual journey. We live on the go, never quite sure where we're going, suspecting there must be an easier path but feeling ourselves somehow always hurled along the bumpiest, most uncertain, and most winding path to everything. The Exodus journey gets at the essence of what it feels like to be an itinerant. We're never quite certain where we are headed, because arriving is not what matters. Going is what is important. Not knowing where we are going forces us to pay attention to where we are. Since we don't know where *there* is, we have to content ourselves with *here*, now, this moment, this spot, this tree, this sound, this breeze, this twist in the road. Even doubts, uncertainty, and wondering if we're going in the right direction or if we heard God right are part of the journey. In the end, not knowing where we are going or how we are going to get there forces us to utterly depend on God.

Women who entered the ministry fifteen years ago, when I was ordained, endured the mocks and jeers of family, friends, and male ministers in order to be ordained and had nothing to look forward to but assignments to a string of some of the smallest, poorest, and most difficult charges in the conference. I avoided the itinerant parish life that many of my sisters accepted and served nobly. But I could not avoid the itinerant inner journey, even though I've never served a church as pastor a day of my life, and haven't stayed around long enough at the annual church conference where assignments are passed out to hear my name mentioned as a possibility for some rural, circuit assignment. While my outward circumstances have tended to be pretty stable and predictable—I have relocated only two or three times since being ordained, and each time at my own initiative—my inner life has been, nevertheless, anything but stable and predictable. Whether it is the itinerant ministry or the itinerant spiritual journey, the commission is the same, and that is to abandon everything—even the place we meant to be going. Those who wish to find themselves must first be willing to lose themselves. Only when we risk getting lost do we find our way, and only when we stop trying to see our footsteps does our pathway become more certain. Encounters with God take place when we set out in a direction we hadn't planned to take and are willing to give up going where we intended to go.

Having made their bold escape out of Egypt and wandered aimlessly for some time through the wilderness, the runaway Hebrew slaves are unsure what direction to take. With the pharaoh and the full force of his impressive chariotry in hot pursuit in the distance, the runaway slaves stagger to the banks of the Red Sea, exhausted and weeping. Before them is nothing but sea. Some slaves begin to cry and complain bitterly to Moses that they should never have struck out on a suicide mission, that it would have been better to have just remained in Egypt and let things be. Moses, on the outside the ever-calm leader, tries to console and reassure the people that they are going right and that deliverance is at hand. On the inside he has doubts himself and isn't sure where to turn next. He is in as much panic as the next Hebrew. He whispers under his breath his own anguished prayer to God for direction. And then comes a voice ringing above the noise, "Why do you cry out to me? Tell the people to go forward." You can be sure that wherever the right place, the appointed place, is, it is *forward*, one step ahead, where you can't see, out in the deep water. There. See? Of course not. You won't see until you go.

Chapter Three

The Mystery of Marriage and Mothering

Behold, I Show You a Mystery

Eventually it comes to you: the thing that makes you exceptional is also what makes you lonely.

LORRAINE HANSBERRY

Some memories you never recover from. Whether you were the agent in a memory's unfolding or were an unintended but inescapable victim of its outcome, the memory remains fresh in your mind as though it occurred yesterday. Perhaps the memory isn't rooted in an event but in a chance meeting, a conversation overheard, a secret that stumbled on you, leaving you reeling from the revelation and permanently different from the person you were before. Or perhaps it is the memory of a dream that found itself in your unconscious, that was hilarious in the way it patched together bits and pieces of your life that, on the surface, had nothing to do with one another but on second thought possibly had everything to do with one another. Or perhaps that dream was terrifying in the way it tapped into your deepest, most unexamined fears. Regardless, the dream's effects remain with you long after you've ceased remembering the actual details. Long after the dream was dreamed, the conversation was exchanged, the event took place, you continue to live with the impact. You keep coming back to it over and over again. You try not to obsess over it, though you have every right to, given its intensity. You try to move on, get over it, live beyond it, whatever those things mean. But you keep coming back to it as a pivotal moment, benchmark, defining moment of who you are.

"Eventually it comes to you," wrote the playwright Lorraine Hansberry in a journal entry more than thirty years old. I wish that were so. Sometimes the bits and pieces of the memory and the dream never come together to make sense. They remain fragments of words, images, and emotions that get embedded in my psyche with no apparent meaning. What does all this mean? I inquire in vain. When will I figure it out? I wonder. How long is "eventually"? Longer than thirty years, evidently, since I continue to find myself reliving and remembering, but not being able to make sense of, the day my mother walked away from me, my four siblings, and our father. The truth is that I can't remember a thing about that day. Blank. I can't even recall whether I was home the day she packed her things and took a taxi to some undisclosed destination across town. I just remember the effects her leaving had on me and on my sisters and brothers (though each of us reacted to her leaving and was changed permanently by it in a curiously different way). Nonetheless, this one simple long-ago occurrence that happened in the life of a thirteen-year-old girl in Atlanta continues to have ripple effects in her life more than thirty years later. Every book and article she writes, whether academic or inspirational, every sermon she preaches, whether good or bad, and every song she sings to her daughter at night when the little one must be returned to her bed after a night walk—whether the song is made up or drawn from memory—represents the attempt of a woman no longer thirteen to make sense of what happened in her life thirty years ago.

The memory of that fateful day back in the sixties continues to assert itself in my imagination, and there doesn't seem to be a thing I can do about it. Each time I try pinning it down in my mind, my heart, whether directly or indirectly, I hope I learn something new about what it means to be myself rather than the self I have tried on and taken off hundreds of times over the years. I also hope I have something important and wise to share with family, friends, and the audiences that continue to be touched by what I'm thinking about life, about love, about pain and disappointments, and above all, about grace. Ironical, isn't it? Our deepest, most painful wounds not only leave us with scars that we bear forever but also, if we make our peace with them, leave us wiser, stronger, more sensitive than we otherwise would have been had we not been afflicted with them. Whoever I am, whoever others think I am, and—certainly—whoever God knows me actually to be is tied and tangled up in the story of a mother forced to make the inconceivable choice back in 1967 to leave her children, her husband, and (most poignantly) the little girl who by all accounts favored her.

While considerable more media attention is spent on exploring the breach between fathers and sons than the one between mothers and their daughters, a Greek poet as far back as the seventh century B.C.E. understood how earth-shattering a daughter's alienation from her mother could be, and set out to write the Eleusinian myth of Demeter and Persephone. The story reenacts the loss and torment a mother and daughter experience when they are separated in heart as much as in body. Don't be fooled, the poet reminds us, the world will pay for separating mothers and daughters.

While out picking the fragrant narcissus flower, Persephone (or Kore) is snatched and taken into the underworld by Hades, the god of the abyss, who holds her hostage there, raping and abusing her in all likelihood. Her mother, Demeter, who refuses to be comforted, is so bereft that, as goddess of the earth, she refuses to let anything grow. Zeus, when he sees all the men and animals who are killed for lack of vegetation and crops, persuades Hades to return Persephone. Psychologically the story celebrates the emotional renewal and intimacy between mothers and daughters; upon reuniting with Persephone, Demeter is so overjoyed that she makes the ground fertile again and bestows the gift of grain and the gift of mysteries upon the Greek people.

The story of Demeter's unrelenting search for her daughter and her refusal to take *no* from a male god, the lengths she went to get her daughter back, and her determination to be reunited with Persephone whatever the cost is comforting to someone who cannot get enough mother love. I would prefer having memories of a mother like Demeter (who was confident, resourceful, and stable enough to rescue her daughter, raise her, and nurture her into womanhood) than those that I do have—of a mother who was always at a loss how to protect her older daughter. I would gladly exchange the wisdom, strength, and sensitivity I have gained from surviving the loss of my mother's abandonment for good, satisfying memories of being rescued by my mother. But unlike the goddesses in the Eleusinian myth, I can't change my fate.

Collecting, hoarding, stockpiling things is the stuff of childhood. These days my daughter is fascinated with crayons and must have nine different shades of every color of the rainbow. I didn't know there were so many shades of purple. Some children acquire an appetite for collecting stamps, dolls, and sports memorabilia. I have acquired a taste for stories about runaway mothers, absent mothers, ailing mothers, flawed mothers, outrageous mothers—which explains why, of the many books I have read over the years, the ones that fasten themselves to my mind and refuse to let go are those about daughters suffering mother loss. Books by daughters who have been left to rummage through their mothers' lives in order to survive the loss of their mothers have their own special shelf in my study: *The Autobiography of My Mother* by Jamaica Kincaid, *Father Melancholy's Daughter* by Gail Godwin, *The Joy Luck Club* by Amy Tan, *Pushed Back to Strength* by Gloria Wade Gayle, *Motherless Daughters* by Hope Edelman, *The Bridges of Madison County* by Robert James Waller, *The Bad Daughter* by Julie Hilden, and a host of others. Despite all the mother-loss books I have whimpered through and all the films on the same topic that have left me weeping uncontrollably in theaters or gnawing on my pillow in front of my television set, my need to figure *exactly, fully, again* why my mother made the choice she did remains. My favorite books and films assure me that I am not crazy, overwrought, or alone in knowing that when a mother leaves, part of her daughter's soul goes with her.

I have flip-flopped over the years between being angry at God (the gods) for allowing my mother to abandon me and blaming myself for not being the kind of daughter a mother would want to stay and protect. But as always, in anger and in guilt the truth looks simple. But it is not. It is far more complex. It's as complex as knowing three decades later that God did not will my mother to walk out on her family and probably didn't try to change her mind. Leaving was her fate. Generations of abuse in her family and years of having no outlet to talk about it left her no choice as a frightened, defeated woman but to leave when the time came to decide. My mother left, and for good reasons I've discovered over the years. But to say that God didn't make my mother leave is not to say that God wasn't present in her leaving. God was present, like a weaver spinning a complex but fanciful pattern on her loom, offering her, me, and our family the possibility of healing and laughter beyond our pain. That's as close to what faith means to me as I can think of—that is, learning to make peace with all that has happened to me in the past, but especially what happened at thirteen, and trying to wrest from that past a blessing for me, my family, and those who look to me. Sometimes we think God is silent when in fact we are the ones who remain silent to God by our refusal to listen to what our memories are trying to tell us.

Of course, some days I think I'm healed from the memory of my mother leaving us. But then something happens to snatch me down under, beneath the tide. The death in June 1997 of Malcolm X's widow, Dr. Betty Shabazz, was one such event. I thought I was back to being thirteen years old again.

But it wasn't so much Dr. Shabazz's death itself that got to me, although it broke my heart to discover that a warrior who had survived so many other battles would die such a tragic death. She died from burns in a fire set by a grandson named in honor of his mythic grandfather, Malcolm X. A twisted, cruel irony, if ever there was one. What sent me spiraling downward into my own painful memories, however, was that Betty Shabazz died leaving motherless (and orphaned) six beautiful, wounded daughters. I sat transfixed to the television watching Athallah, the eldest, stand outside the hospital and announce her mother's passing: "My father lived strong, my mother died honorably. And now we must adapt to living a life without parents." Her voice cracked several times, and so did my heart. I studied the faces of Shabazz's daughters and relived my own loss decades earlier. We think we've gotten over the past and then something happens that lets us know we haven't gotten over it: we've just outlived it. But the memory, the sting, the sorrow never lags far behind; it sneaks up and seizes us at the most unlikely times, taking no thought that we're too weary to think about it or too parched spiritually to find any worth in it. But there it is, demanding a hearing. We try to straighten up, pay attention, and let it have some small say again. For that is yet again, I suppose, how God speaks to us through memory—in bits and pieces, some small insight here, some small insight there. Every time it pops up in our psyches, we're supposed to learn something we hadn't discovered before, until eventually, years, perhaps decades, later, a mosaic of understanding that brings healing and sometimes even laughter overwhelms us.

When a friend recommended a book about a baby bird combing the countryside in search of his mother as good bedtime reading for my daughter, I promptly went out and bought it. A baby bird hatches and comes into the world alone and embarks on a perilous journey in search of its mother. Despite appearances, however, the baby bird is not motherless. The mother bird took off moments before the baby bird hatched, in an anxious search for food. (There's no mention of the father bird.) Hatched and hungering for a mother figure, the baby bird tumbles from its nest and sets out from one creature to the next and from animals to inanimate objects in search of its mother. Not knowing for sure who or what to look for, not knowing his own kind, but driven by the need to connect and to be nurtured, the bird greets the kitten, hen, dog, and cow, among others, with the same plaintive question: "Are you my mother?" (which is also the book's title).

I was as hooked on reading the book as my daughter was on hearing it read. The baby bird's question struck a chord in me. But one day when I noticed that my daughter was becoming inconsolable every time she overheard that I had to go out of town, I knew that the time had come to retire our favorite book. It was time to make her understand that there are different kinds of leaving, even though the author never bothers to make the distinction. There's a difference between a mother going to work (like the mother bird and me) and a mother going away for good (like my mother): that was my daughter's lesson.

But in a lesson for a then three-year-old was enfolded a revelation for her then forty-something mother. There is a difference between a mother leaving her daughter because she doesn't love her and a mother leaving a vicious cycle of abuse and neglect that makes her think she is unfit, incapable of caring for her five children whether she stays or leaves.

"Eventually it comes to you": what wounds us the deepest has also the power to bless us most profoundly. This is, as one writer put it, a saving mystery. Reversals occur in unexpected quarters. Whoever I have become—certainly the bad parts, but also the very, very good stuff—can be directly traced back to my mother walking out of our home thirty years ago. But whoever I have become is also more than the trauma of that memory. Also at work in me have been the gifts of love, patience, humor, tears, and dignity that were planted in me by other women (and men) sent by God to soothe my pain. What I, my sister, and my brothers lost when our mother left can never be fully tallied, and most certainly never recaptured. But what I and they found in one another, and in the people, church, and community that welcomed us motherless children, can never be taken away from us either.

Blessings cost just as certainly as blessings bless; and this, I think, is what Lorraine Hansberry had in mind in her 1963 journal entry. Whatever wisdom, strength, and sensitivity there is to be discovered comes about as a result of our first being willing to take our secrets out of the trunk where we hide them from ourselves and to look at them, to look at the stories buried there. Remembering the past, thinking back through one's mother (or father) to restitch one's own life, returning over and over again to a memory that can't be escaped, is a blessing, says Frederick Buechner, because it offers you the second, third, fourth, fifth chance to bless the past through memory and to be blessed by it. If you're luckier than I was, it won't take thirty years for *it* to *come to you.* But if you're anything like me you'll be happy to know it's never too late to run your finger over the seams that unite the patches of experiences you've had and finally see the way those experiences have been woven inextricably together by a master weaver who was all the while, quietly and unobtrusively, fashioning a self for you, unbeknownst to you.

Mother's Day

So as a parent I wanted to make sure you had all your physical needs met and a lot of love. But as a parent I could not ignore other people's children or pain that spills over to public space and threatens the safety and quality of life and pocketbook and future of every American. I also wanted to make sure I left you a community and future more safe and hopeful than the one inherited, and an example of one person trying to make a difference.

MARIAN WRIGHT EDELMAN

Had I not already peeped in on my daughter through the one-way glass that day, when I came to her classroom to pick her up, and seen already that indeed she was alive and healthy, the tone of her teacher's words—"Renita, we need to talk"—would have sent me into a panic. As it was, my knees buckled. I could see from my daughter's cartwheels and squeals that she was fine and in one piece, and even delighted to see me as I walked through the door. But teachers with grave expressions on their faces have been known to make a mother's heart sink. I braced myself for bad news, a scolding, a threat, a payment reminder, a dreaded update. The teacher beckoned me to join her at her desk, while one of the aides escorted my daughter off to play in home center.

"I thought you should know that Savannah is biting and acting out aggressively in school these days. I have had a talk with her already, but I thought that after three days of repeated biting, it was time for you as her mother to be informed."

"Is that right?" I stood there stunned and widemouthed. I didn't know what else to say. Relieved that it wasn't as bad as I had thought, still I was shocked at the news that my daughter was boring her teeth into another child's flesh.

My fantasies about having a daughter never included one that bit other children. "I feed her in the mornings," I wanted to say, but decided against it. My daughter biting another mother's daughter—I couldn't think of what I'd done to drive her to this. (Mothers have a way of viewing flaws in their children as a reflection of some inherent defect in themselves, which explains why teachers have the power to make mothers become apoplectic.) At times like these I miss having a mother to call for advice. "Lord, help," I mutter under my breath.

The day-care teacher proceeded to tell me that when my daughter's playmate refused Savannah her doll or refused to let Savannah slide first, Savannah used her teeth to tear into the child's flesh—first the face, then the hand, finally the forearm of a twenty-month-old little girl. "Rebecca has gone home three days in the past week with wounds from Savannah." Of course, the child's mother was upset, the teacher reminded me. Of course she's upset, I thought. I would be murderous if it were the other way around.

"I have sent Savannah to time-out, I've made her hug and apologize to Rebecca, and I have scolded her; but it's obvious that it's time for a conference with you."

I looked over at my pint-size daughter, who by now had made her way over to our conference table and was wrapping herself around my leg. She knew she was in trouble and stared intently up at me with her thumb in her mouth, her 2T jumper soiled, her tiny white sneakers scuffed, and her thick dark hair pulled away from her face into a bunny tail. God made sure that every child was outfitted with just enough charms and adorable looks to protect them from the first impulse of outraged parents.

"Savannah?" I called her name softly and inquisitively. I was talking to the teacher, asking, in effect: "Do you mean my child? Not my child! Are you sure you have the right child? You must be confusing my child with some other child"—or some other dumb statement parents are wont to say when they are in denial. My daughter looked up into my eyes. She sucked harder on a thumb and looked away.

By now the teacher was waiting patiently for my response.

I decided against the obvious one spoken by mothers the world over: "I don't know where she got that from."

"Has Rebecca's mommy picked her up yet?" I asked.

The teacher shook her head and pointed to a hefty little figure standing across the room by herself, playing with the toy computer. She seemed fine to me. But there was no over-looking the purple mark on her pale skin. "Is that her?" I said to the teacher as our eyes met. She nodded.

"Rebecca?" I began approaching the little girl slowly and softly, so as not to frighten her. I stretched my arms out when she turned her head in my direction. "Come here, baby." I pulled up a rocking chair that was nearby and sat in it. Savannah was by my side with her thumb in her mouth.

A stocky little white girl with pale, pale skin and mousy brown hair looked curiously in my direction. She hesitated for a moment when her eyes fell on Savannah, but when she saw the rocking chair and the gentle gesture of my arms, she tottered calmly over into my direction. The little white child climbed up into my lap without reservation and relaxed her hand on the fold in my arm and stared up at me with a calm expression. For a girl almost two years old, Rebecca had a solid frame. She didn't appear a bit confused about what I wanted, what she was supposed to do, or what was next. Like most children, she trusted me to do the right thing in a rock-ing chair. The other five children in the classroom gathered around us, looking on with curiosity.

Savannah began whimpering as she watched me cuddling Rebecca in my arms and snuggled up to my lap, trying to climb aboard. Both little girls shifted, wiggled, and adjusted themselves in my lap, each looking at the other with caution, neither one saying a word to the other. Now there were two little girls in my lap, one brown and my own, the other white and belonging to someone else. What would I do next? It dawned on me that this was my first time holding a white child in my arms. I was amazed at how natural the little white girl felt in my lap. My eyes fell on the bruises my daughter had inflicted on the little white girl, and I was filled with shame.

I bent down to kiss Rebecca's bruises. Savannah tried to distract me by pulling my face over into her direction. I kissed her forehead and kissed Rebecca's too.

The natural thing to do in a rocking chair is to rock, so I rocked. I decided against lecturing two-year-olds. The safest thing to do would be simply to sing.

"Jesus loves the little children, all the children of the world. Red and yellow, black and white, they are precious in his sight. Jesus loves the little children of the world."

Rebecca was Jewish, I later discovered. But for that one moment, neither she nor I nor Savannah nor history, and certainly not Jesus, cared.

The Grace of Daily Obligation

Some women wait for something
to change and nothing
does change
so they change themselves.

AUDRE LORDE

In a book with such a complex history, filled with confounding customs and perplexing rationalizations, capable of arousing astonishing reactions and maddening behavior, it may seem ridiculous to call attention to one passage as being particularly irksome. Competition in the Bible for the most exasperating passages is stiff. But as a woman, a minister, and a professor specializing in the first thirty-nine books of the canon, I find myself routinely in the position of having to defend, explain, or comment on some portions of the Bible that can only be described kindly as abstruse. Often it's the believer in me who demands the scholar in me to make sense of some irritating passage of scripture. A vexing verse in the book of Genesis comes up regularly for cross-examination: *"And when the Lord saw that Leah was hated, the Lord opened her womb"* (Genesis 29:31).

Other passages, better known and more widely used, have left women (and some men) apoplectic and scurrying for goddesses. But this one has been known to send me hurling the Bible at the moon. It remains, as far as I am concerned, one of the most infuriating verses in the entire Bible. I wish I could get my hands on the writer and shake him. "What in the world does hate have to do with childbearing?" I want to ask. "Since when is having numerous children the answer to a loveless marriage?" I want to know. I suppose I could ask God. But God isn't speaking to me just now. I have to direct my protests to whoever authored these texts.

"Why didn't God simply make Jacob love Leah?" asked a woman belonging to a Genesis study group I once directed. "Better yet," added another, a single mother of two, "why didn't God fix it so that Leah didn't care whether or not Jacob loved her?" I was proud of the group of six women who came out weekly to study the book of Genesis with me. But I'm afraid we were outnumbered when I think of all the harm verses like this one has done to women, to abused women, to mothers, to children born in loveless marriages. I want to rip the page from the Bible.

If ever there was an occasion when God could have made a profound, unequivocal statement about relationships, about betrayal, about abuse, about power—I think to myself—here was one. But no such statement was made. Surely the inference isn't supposed to be that having babies is the remedy to a loveless marriage. Passages like this stand behind the maledictions of provincial men like the fifth-century North African bishop Augustine, who argued women's inferiority to men, and the sixteenth-century Protestant Reformer Martin Luther, who, arguing for something like a justification of vocation, insisted that women find their hope and their salvation in childbearing. But what does a passage like this mean for the many women who, for a variety of reasons, never give birth to children?

A passage hopelessly provincial in its attempt to describe the plight of an unloved woman and infuriatingly patriarchal in its attitude toward women's role in the material and spiritual universe—what are we to do with a passage like this? the women in my study group were left to ponder. *"And when the Lord saw that Leah was hated, the Lord opened her womb."* Was it possible to make sense of an irritating verse like this one a few years back when I sat nursing my three-month-old daughter at my sore breasts? Had I colluded with patriarchy by having my daughter? I wondered. Strangling from the smell of my own milk, stranded in a nursery that doubled as my study, and knee deep in diapers, had I become my own enemy? I asked myself. Before pregnancy, I was a biblical scholar, a minister, a writer, I would remind myself, a woman who had succeeded in carving out a place for herself in a triad of professions that tended to reward only those who succeeded in detaching themselves from the obligations of love, children, and domesticity. Each of the three professions I'd chosen for myself called for a celibacy of heart to be productive, an ability to close the door on the world for hours of concentration and not feel guilty about the hue and cry on the other side. And I had had such a heart—before. But now I was a scholar, a minister, a writer, and *also* a mother, as a friend pointed out. And that *also* made me more like Leah in the book of Genesis than I cared to admit.

I looked down at my young daughter, who was looking gratefully and hungrily into my eyes, and I knew instinctively that gone were my days of being able to barricade myself in my study for hours on end, shunning human interaction, refusing to talk to people, ignoring the invitations by spouse and friends to eat, bathe, play, or sleep. I had worked so hard for so long to prove that I had what it took to make it in the predominantly male professions I had chosen, enduring the long lonely hours of study; it struck panic into me to think that my ability to keep up the pace of my profession was being slowly sucked out of me by the child on my breast.

With an infant attached to me who felt permanently affixed to my chest cavity, whose hunger for my voice, my touch, and even my scent felt bottomless, I knew instinctively that now as *also* a mother I couldn't continue to value detachment and solitude as the imperatives for the contemplative life. I'd have to find a new way of thinking about the obligations that now faced me as a mother and search out role models for combining solitude and intimacy. I wanted to believe that it was possible both to engage in fulfilling work as a minister, scholar, and writer and to find satisfaction in the daily obligations of mothering. But at the moment I felt like Leah, too drained of energy and time to figure out how quickly blessings can turn into burdens.

Looking back on the days before my daughter's birth, I am amazed at how little I reflected on the tensions that were already arising from juggling work and marriage. I was perfectly prepared to believe that my husband's resentment of my work and his complaints about my ability to detach for days on end and to retreat into whatever world I created for myself so as to write books, articles, and speeches was a failure on his part. While his work as a pastor of a growing congregation kept him busy and made his hours unstable, still he had the remarkable ability to be present to wherever he was at the moment—which, of course, was why I fell in love with him in the first place, but which also meant that when he finally got home after a day of visiting the sick, counseling the bereaved, praying at banquets, teaching Bible study, presiding over committee meetings, he was home and ready to be home—until the phone rang (which, of course, was often, in a pastor's home). The problem was that the contemplative writer is never home; she's always off in her head chasing down ideas, reading or thinking about reading, writing or thinking about writing. As for my part in our endless arguments during that time, it never dawned on me that I needed to rethink whether it would be possible to remain wedded to *this* man and continue to write and research in ways I'd grown accustomed to. I never thought about the growing irresolvable tensions in my marriage and work but chose with every complaint lodged by my husband to remain resolute in my belief that he would just have to adjust. "You've got one job," I'd yell from the other side of my study; "I've got three."

And then came motherhood, and with it a fourth job.

My husband would just have to learn how to fend for himself until his wife returned from the world of books, but I couldn't expect a young child to do the same. When my eyes first fell on her screaming, grayish, twisting body in the delivery room and I fell moronically in love with her, I knew the time had come to find new ways to be a contemplative.

There's nothing natural about mothering, just as there's nothing natural about writing or being a minister (or being a wife, for that matter). They are all inhuman tasks that require colossal amounts of concentration. Within six months, having a baby had wreaked havoc on my professional life, draining me of the energies and time I needed to think and to read. With only two or three hours a night of sleep, it became difficult to sit for hours concentrating on an idea, sniffing out a subject, walking back and forth around a thought, and trying to chase down a hunch. With the increasing demands of motherhood and the mounting pressures in those early years of a pending tenure review, I felt as if I was being torn apart, dismantled, put back together again (but never in a way that felt right to me), only to be left ripped up in the end and left in a heap. Having a baby crying in the bassinet next to my bed, nursing every three hours, changing diapers every other minute, changing and washing the same clothes all day, with a growing accumulation of baby *stuff* crowding my space, and having simultaneously to put the final touches on a book and to keep up with class lectures, I was often tottering on the edge. The only thing I had to draw from were the index cards of ideas I had tucked away from my childless days; they pulled me through the writing and speaking necessary for a successful tenure review.

Having a child not only makes grits of my brain; it poses a mixed blessing to my prayer life and spiritual journey. Enormous amounts of time are diverted away not only from my work but also from prayer, meditation, study, and attuning my ear to an inner voice. Through the ages every mystic writing about what it means to live consciously before the sacred has argued that contemplation begins with the willingness and ability to endure extended periods of silence. On my night table lie four books filled with quotes by mystics and poets on the gift of contemplation. But with a toddler around I have been reduced to reading in snatches what they have to say about the contemplative journey. Of the four books on my night table I notice that three are written by men. (This may be telling, but since mine is hardly a scientific sampling, the authors' gender in this instance may be utterly beside the point.)

"Nothing will change the fact that I cannot produce the least thing without absolute solitude," wrote Goethe. On the silence that derives from the monastic life, wrote Thomas Merton, "My life is a listening, His is a speaking. My salvation is to hear and respond. For this, my life must be silent. Hence, my silence is my salvation." And from a man who obviously had a phobia against toddlers, Chief Standing Bear: "A child who cannot sit still is a half-developed child." As a woman and a mother I am floored that men have applauded and have gotten away with such sayings. The inference is clear: without solitude and silence it is impossible to experience the creative powers of divine mystery. Without silence one cannot hear one's self think. Without solitude one does not have the privilege of luxuriating on a thought and seeing where, if anywhere, it might lead. But I've learned, like many women and caregivers, that even without solitude and silence it *is* possible to encounter the sacred. Relationships, obligation, connectedness, intimacy, and love can also be channels of sacred mystery. Isn't this the message of not only women such as Leah in the book of Genesis, but thousands of women and men over the centuries who've given themselves away in nursing the sick, caring for children, and taking care of the needy?

But I can't find a single male in the books next to my bed who thinks so. Some of the women writing about silence and solitude seem to recognize this point. In a tiny collection of quotes on silence and solitude, women writing on the topic seem to get the connection between loving and mystery. The poet May Sarton, who, though childless, lived a full and conscious life, wrote eloquently in her journals about the need to strike a balance between relationships and solitude:

> I am here alone for the first time in weeks, to take up my "real" life again at last. That is what is strange—that friends, even passionate love, are not my real life unless there is time alone in which to explore and to discover what is happening or has happened. Without the interruptions, nourishing and maddening, this life would become arid. Yet I taste it fully only when I am alone.

There is also my favorite, by Stephanie Dowrick: "The capacity to be comfortably alone flows from satisfying experiences of being with someone else. What's more, satisfying experiences of being with someone else fuel a continuing capacity to be alone, without feeling adrift or lonely."

If my devotions were confined to what men write, I'd feel defeated. But I read these quotes by women and feel somewhat encouraged. It may just be possible to be a writer and a mother, a scholar and a mother, and God forbid, a minister. Having lived more years unmarried than married, longer childless than with a child, I know full well the benefits of having uninterrupted time to think and pray. But after six years of marriage and a short time of being *also* a mother, I've discovered as well the mystery that awaits one who shares herself in mothering, loving, and caring. I don't want to give up one for the other. Angels have been known to visit mothers, nurses, and caregivers. One may not have the time to stop and give them a meal, but still it's possible to give them a nod.

Laden as she later was with four male children and a phi-landering husband, Leah evidently experienced something of an encounter with eternity (above the din of screaming chil-dren, a loveless marriage, and unending chores) that pro-pelled her at one point in the story to say, "This time I will praise the Lord!" We can only speculate about what hap-pened. Her male narrator never says. But then, that is to be expected. Men are always clueless as to what makes a woman finally say, "Enough!"

Before I can finish typing the first draft of a manuscript, the phone rings. I tell myself not to answer, wonder if the answer-ing machine is on, and normally wouldn't answer if I lived alone, but I answer anyway because always in the back of my head I wonder if it might be an emergency call from my daughter's school. The writing is going badly anyway. The voice on the other end is one of my husband's church mem-bers, hysterical and crying. "He's not at home." I try to sound warm, but not too concerned, lest the distraught member on the other line decide that one minister is as good as another.

"It's mama, Reverend Renita. I think she's getting ready to leave us." I recognize the voice and remember that her mother is under hospice care. The older woman has cancer of the spine. I dread the next question: "Can you come over?"

No, no, no, I can't come! So, why am I in my car driving across town to a little clapboard house on a corner? And why am I muttering to myself, "I'm not the pastor," as I step to the front door? And what use is there in saying, "I know I'm a minister, but I don't want to be here. I've got a book to finish. It's my day to pick up Savannah from the day care," when I'm already in the sick woman's bedroom?

The smell of dying flesh is throughout the room. I'm a teacher precisely because I don't do death watches, I think to myself as I come closer to the dying woman's bed.

"Mama, the minister is here," the daughter whispers in her mother's ear. I try to look comforting and reverent, but I don't open my mouth because I don't know what to say. The frail dark, dark woman with a halo of curly black hair is lying quietly beneath a patchwork quilt. The quilt is pulled up to her neck, and only her tiny head shows from beneath the blanket. Her shallow breath sends faint ripples through the quilt. I am amazed at how smooth and beautiful the woman's skin is on her sunken face. She reminds me of an old jar of molasses my great-grandmother kept high up on a kitchen cabinet out of the reach of tiny hands. The lid on the jar was so old it had begun to rust, but my great-grandmother wouldn't hear of breaking the seal. Knowing that molasses was her favorite, my late grandfather had gone out after one of their spats and bought the jar of molasses for her when he was trying to make up. Whenever one of us, her many grandchildren, pestered her about opening up the molasses, she always refused, saying, "More in that jar than simply molasses. There's memories stored in there as well."

"Mama, the minister is here," the young woman says again, more for my sake than for her mother's sake. I've seen death enough to know that the woman is getting ready to "travel," a term used by Southerners to describe the final stage of transitioning, when the dying, drifting somewhere between life and the hereafter, begin slipping deeper and deeper into a coma. Her breathing is hard and erratic, her eyes slightly opened.

I've accompanied my husband on visits like this a number of times and usually stand back quietly watching as he calmly, gently, unfalteringly takes the hands of the dying and rubs them, strokes their hair with one hand and reads the Bible with the other, laughs and prays with those with the temperament, sings and prays with those who lack it. I tag along for moral support. I hand him the Bible, when he needs me to, or hug and console members of the family, if needed. But this time I'm alone. I forgot to bring my Bible.

The daughter looks to me for words. The only thing that comes to mind is an old spiritual I heard elderly people at my church sing during prayer time and at funerals when I was a child. I don't know if I remember all the words, but it's all that comes to mind. I clear my throat and try to remember how it goes. *"Throw out the life line."* My raspy tenor voice cracks. *"Throw out the life line. Someone is drifting away. Throw out the life line. Throw out the life line. Someone is drifting today."*

After fifteen minutes of singing my throat is dry, but I'm too afraid to stop, lest I have to think of something on my own to say. I point to my throat, and the daughter steps out of the room to go to the kitchen. A minute passes and I'm fresh out of music. I rub the old woman's hand as I've seen my husband do times before, but my mind is not on what's going on in the room. I'm thinking about the things I've left piled on my desk: the notes for my eight o'clock Hebrew class the next morning, a load of clothes to wash, phone calls to return, a manuscript to finish.

"Is today tomorrow?"

I look down to see the older woman staring intently up at the ceiling. Her eyes never meet mine, but it's apparent that she's waiting for me to answer.

"Mam?"

I am too stunned to even remember her name. I pull my hand back frightened.

"Is today tomorrow?" she asks once more.

"No mam. Today is Thursday." I wasn't sure what she was asking.

Shaking her head as if to let me know that I didn't get it,

and perhaps annoyed a bit at my ignorance, the woman rolls her eyes to the back of her head and closes the lids over her eyes.

What was she asking? What kind of question was that? What did she mean, is today tomorrow? By the time the daughter returns with a glass of water, I am reaching for my sunglasses and making motions to go. I give her some excuse about needing to pick up my daughter from school and promise to let my husband know that he should come straight over as soon as possible. She thanks me for coming and assures me that her mother would be happy to know my concern for her.

Is today tomorrow? The dying woman's question has shaken me. It stays with me the rest of the day, the week. I turn it over in my mind one way and then another as one would an interesting urn one happened upon at a flea market, hoping to ascertain its value.

God speaks to us through the stuff of our lives and through the stuff of other people's lives also. We hardly recognize it as God when it takes place, and rarely are able to decipher what, if anything, it all means. Days, weeks, often years go by before we figure it out, if we ever do. Part of the reason we completely miss both God and the message is that we expect God in lofty places. We expect God to appear in those places where holy men usually conduct their affairs. If God speaks, it will be on mountains, in caves, in sanctuaries, in temples, in the cloister of one's study, in classrooms, in the library, where we're surrounded by books—anywhere but in a nursery, on a playground, in a kitchen, in a parking lot, at the checkout counter, or at the bedside of a decaying old woman. God shows up only where silence is cultivated, solitude is appreciated, and abstinence is the rule, we're told—not while we hold a frail body steady as it stoops over the toilet, or amid noisy children, or as we're driving down a busy freeway. But the lessons of holy women run counter to such a claim. And we have missed them. We have missed whatever redemption there is to be found in stories about women like Leah, and other, dying women. We are bereft because we lack traditions that elevate caring for children, the aged, and the infirmed to meaningful venues for encountering spiritual wisdom. Our society views caring as an impediment that squanders our potential and ties us down. It demeans mothering, underpays day-care workers and teachers, and penalizes adults who take time off to care for aging parents.

But in the life of a loveless, lactating woman named Leah, a mirror is held up so that we might see ourselves—our failures, our lovelessness, and our opportunities for grace. In her story we discover how the interruptions of life, and nurturing and caring, can bring us into deeper encounters with God. The story reclaims the ordinary, routine, mundane, unspectacular work of being faithful to love. It's what in some circles is referred to as "the grace of daily obligation": glimpsing something you've never glimpsed before about your self, a loved one, the past, an old wound, the present, while performing the routine, unspectacular acts of trying to serve faithfully those you care about; turning down the opportunity to give (what you think is) that once-in-a-lifetime chance to speak in Calcutta because you already promised to take the kids, along with your aging father, to Disneyland that week. (And there at Disneyland seven months later, glancing over at the smile on your father's face and seeing the glee on your kid's face, you remember why you promised to do Disneyland in the first place.)

What I enjoy most about stories like Leah's (and is a feature common to many biblical stories of women) is that there is no divine intervention. Angels do not appear out of nowhere to direct the way; there are no miracles, no voices out of the whirlwind. Men retreat to mountains, take refuge in temples, leave home to journey far away, or sequester themselves from family and friends to think and pray, while women are left to encounter God, angels, and the sacred in the daily routine of caring and giving.

"Is today tomorrow?" the old woman asked no one in particular, but me especially. Standing over her bed, my mind racing with all the things I'd left at home undone, I felt the brush of an angel across my brow. Is today tomorrow? No. Today is today. And tomorrow is somewhere out there, unknown and unknowable, where dreams are formed. I think of the old lady's question whenever I think I ought to be doing anything other than what I am doing at the time or ought to be somewhere other than where I am at the time.

Having babies still is not a remedy for a loveless marriage. I don't think anyone, not even I, a Genesis scholar, can come up with anything clever that can excuse or detract from the story's sorrowful claim. In the hands of those looking for a rationale for doing so, it still has the potential to justify keeping women tied to loveless, life-depleting unions. Nevertheless, for those of us bent on saving all our stories, even the horrific ones, the story of Leah can serve as a lesson in the holiness of nurturing and caring: it is work that has the potential to open us up to new revelations about self, about life, about God. Flesh rubbing against flesh, soothing and healing it—this humanizes us, opens us up to new insights into ourselves, and teaches us compassion. And ultimately it restores us. A society that spurns the work of caregiving cuts itself off from learning about life itself. Relegating all the caregiving that faces us to spouses, nannies, housekeepers, maids, live-in nurses, and paid personnel threatens to make us overestimate our strengths and can blind us to our own vulnerabilities. We miss the work that can help to civilize us.

It is very difficult to stay up all night rocking a sick child, cooling her fevered brow, changing her soiled linen, rubbing her fragile body with ointments, praying unceasingly for her healing—and return to your corporate suite on the twenty-somethingth floor and sign the order to lay off ten thousand workers. After getting down on your knees to clip the toenails of an infirm parent, combing the hair of a comatose friend, wiping the drool from the mouth of your favorite aunt, who has Alzheimer's, or feeding your grandbaby her first bottle of baby cereal, it's almost impossible to order the bombing of homes in other lands. After listening to the sound of your toddler's erratic breathing all night, it's pretty hard to sit in a Senate chamber and vote for measures that threaten our environment and the health of our children's children.

The grace of daily obligation.

I will never be the writer I would have been had I not become a mother. Nor will I ever be the minister or professor I could have been if I hadn't had to suffer the interruptions of a sulking child or the vibes of a brooding husband transmitted under the door of my study. I give up writing the book I might have written or the sermon I might have preached every time I wander out of my study and follow the smell of popcorn wafting in the air, follow it to the family room, where the rest of the family is watching *The Lion King* for the forty-second time. I'll never be able to recapture the fine sentences swirling in my head, or the fresh revelations that were about to lay hold of me. But for the joy of getting down on the cold hardwood floor and singing, off-key, "Akuna Matata," I'll settle for bits and pieces of revelation God sends my way, and see what, if anything, I can make of them when I can. Because today is today, and it's all I have.

If I Knew Then What I Know Now

As iron sharpens iron, so one person sharpens another.

PROVERBS 27:17

When we decided to get married, both my husband-to-be and I quickly agreed that we had better set about the task of writing our own vows and dispense with the ones outlined in the Book of Common Prayer's Solemnization of Matrimony. We'd both had plenty of occasions in our combined twenty years of ministry to use the vows in the Book of Common Prayer in marriage ceremonies we'd performed, but neither of us was willing to chance our union with the same vows. No way.

Let's face it: at thirty-seven years of age I was simply too old to pledge to love and obey anyone. Likewise, I was too old and it was too late for me to think of entering marriage as a remedy against sin or as a means for procreating children (as the prefatory charge opines). Further, at age thirty-seven, not only had I not been a ward of my father for more than twenty years, but as a grown, thinking woman I couldn't imagine allowing myself being given by my father to my husband like some prize cow.

To complicate things, there was the sensitive matter of all those years of being single. Let's just say that given the number of people we'd both loved, known, and made promises to as single people, some of whom were bound to be at the ceremony because they didn't think we would go through with it (after all, we didn't marry them), we agreed that it would be wise to dispense with inquiries found in the Book of Common Prayer such as "If anyone knows any reason why these two people should not be joined together, let him [or her] speak now or forever hold his [or her] peace."

Fortunately, the couple who officiated at our wedding ceremony were friends of ours and ministers as well, and had considerable experience with tinkering with marriage vows. We took what we thought was the best from a number of traditions, added our own thoughts on the subject, threw them all together, stirred them up for good measure, and gigglingly concluded that we'd outwitted the gods. Seven months into marriage, we both realized that the joke was on us. It became clear that what had taken a few nights of conference calls back and forth, going over words, checking phraseology, and dickering over what we could live with, and what had taken twenty-five minutes *tops* to say in a ceremony was going to take a lifetime to actually live up to. With all the arrogance of the young and all the naiveté of the uninitiated we forswore traditional vows, thinking we knew better what we needed to say to each other and what, after all, as intelligent adults and experienced clergy, we were capable of promising and fulfilling. Each of us was like a densely grown garden: nothing new could be planted unless something else was uprooted and removed. Each of us was in for major reforesting. Repeating the vows we'd written was the easy part. Trying to live up to our vows, daily, constantly, up close, cheek-to-jowl, under the same roof was what was going to chop us up into tiny little pieces.

> Dearly Beloved, we are gathered together here in the sight of God, and in the presence of these witnesses, to join together this man and this woman in holy matrimony; which is an honorable estate, instituted of God . . .

My husband is convinced that God brought the two of us together. I have my suspicions about what he means when he says that. I know what others mean when they say it. It's their corny and naive way of saying what others have believed before—that God, for inscrutable reasons known only to those around at the beginning of time, being idle and bored by all the goings-on in the universe, jumped at the chance to fiddle with history and time to see to it that these two human beings would meet, fall in love, and marry. Comforting to consider, when things are going good; but it's a cruel joke to consider when the marriage is awful. And there is nothing worse than a bad marriage, just as there is nothing better than a good one. Much of marriage entails joining up with someone who will see to it that the rest of your wedded existence will be lived vacillating regularly back and forth between these two extremes.

When my husband says that God brought us together, I twitch. What exactly does he mean? Am I such an irascible person to live with, and he such an infuriatingly difficult person to please—which makes us so unbelievably ill suited for each other—that it must be God's punishment for sins we committed that we should be together and have never lifted a hand to each other?

But even though I smirk at how corny it sounds, I am as

convinced as he is. To think that somewhere in two people's naive reasoning, their lustful groping after each other, and their desperate need to matter to someone was God, who *ultimately, mercifully* consented to use their naive reasoning, their lustful groping, and desperate needs in order to work out some grander, inscrutable purposefulness in it all—why, it's unthinkable.

I am convinced that almost a decade ago, on a fine candlelit evening in August, God was setting me up. Probably glad to be done with my whinings and pleadings that God wasn't as responsive as I'd expected, and disappointed that I assigned much of the blame to God rather than to myself, God "gave" me to my husband with certainty of the results. As usual, God was right. I have never been so serious about recultivating a relationship with God as I have been for almost a decade of marriage. I have learned things about love, fidelity, commitment, gentleness, and forgiveness that simply weren't possible when I was single. There was no compelling reason to do so. But now that I'm smack in the middle of matrimony, trying daily to learn how to love *this* one man, to do it right (and if not right, then, surely, decently), wedlock has driven me straight back to God.

Marriage stripped me of the luxury of hiding who I really am. I can no longer hide from myself, from God, and from another human being. The constant, daily effort to be present, open, honest, transparent, defenseless before another stirs up the urge in me to withdraw and hide. Strange, the push and pull of intimacy, the wanting to be close but not that close, needing to be near but not so near, praying for companionship but not wanting constant company. It makes sense now why the Hebrew prophets used the marriage bond to capture poetically the joys and struggles of the union between God and human beings. I ran away from God because I couldn't bear the intimacy, the accountability, the living under God's constant gaze. And now I find myself scurrying to find my way back to God because I know I need a power greater than my own to stay in this marriage.

. . . which is not to be entered into unadvisedly, but reverently, discreetly, and in the fear of God.

Unadvisedly. Humph. What two people intoxicated with lust and addicted to love bother to listen to good advice when they're bent on knotting their demons together? We tried counseling, sort of; and when it was clear that we'd never marry if we continued, we stopped. Only those who want to *stay* married seek out counseling in the beginning, not those who want to *get* married. Who really knew what lay ahead for us? Some tried to tell us, but we didn't have enough sense to listen. As much as we sympathized with those who tried to warn us, and nodded sympathetically with those who described painstakingly what had gone wrong in their marriage, nevertheless we were certain that our marriage would be different.

No one would ever marry if they really knew what awaited them around the corner, down the way, or at the bend in the road. Better they don't know. Love's job is to dope you up so that you don't notice or care that there's a giant-size trowel aimed at your heart just ahead down the road.

The ministers's warning brought to mind words I am laboring over in a commentary I'm writing on the Song of Solomon: *"Daughters of Jerusalem, I charge you by the gazelles and by the does of the field: Do not arouse or awaken love until it so desires."* The truth is that this is not the first

time I have fallen in love. I have loved and been loved by others. But it was not the right time. Right man, wrong time;
wrong man, right time—until now, that was the story of my
life. And now, finally, the right man at the right time. For sure,
even with the right person it will be a struggle.

> Renita comes to you this day giving you the most precious thing
> any human can give another—her love. She comes saying she be-
> lieves that you deserve her faith and trust and she is willing to
> walk with you through the remainder of her life. I challenge you
> to be worthy of that confidence.

The poor man didn't have a chance. He didn't know what
hit him. How could he know that with my faith, my trust, and
my willingness to walk with him came my fears, my demons,
my bruises, my temper, my moody ways, and my long feet,
one pointing east and the other pointing west? How could I
be so blind as to stand behind those words, to commission
them, in fact? What was I thinking? (Probably wondering if
the caterer had delivered the wedding cake at the house as
promised.) And to think that I consented to take on his fears,
demons, demanding ways—it's hard to believe.

What an incredible risk the two of us took. I risked letting
a complete stranger see me naked. And he pledged the same
to me.

To be married is to live stark naked before another human
being. The union of Adam and Eve in Eden was based on just
such a notion of mutual nakedness: "And the two were both
naked and not ashamed." Now, when the closest to love you
know anything about is the lust in your loins, then the
prospect of seeing the other person walk around naked all
the time doesn't sound like a bad prospect. But the nakedness

the biblical writers were thinking about is not as literal as that. It's worse. It's living completely shorn, unadorned, stripped of pretenses, wide open, and deprived of all the pennyante excuses you've relied upon in the past to excuse your behavior. It's the kind of nakedness that leaves you daily defenseless and scared out of your mind. What if . . . ? We risked that we wouldn't laugh at each other's nakedness. We risked that when the truth about us came out, we wouldn't despise each other. We risked that even if we were disappointed that the other was not what we'd imagined, we would not walk away from the truth.

No one consciously plans to live life that naked to the world, but in marriage there's nowhere to hide. And to think that many people prepare to leap off such a cliff using physical attraction as their barometer that it's safe to jump. Absurd.

Be well assured that if these solemn vows are kept inviolate, as God's word demands, and if you steadfastly endeavor to do the will of your heavenly Creator, God will bless your marriage, will grant you fulfillment in it, and will establish your home in peace.

If, if, if—a few months into the marriage we'd already broken those vows a hundred times. Sleeping with another person would have been the kindest thing we could have done to each other. But we chose the crueler route. We've fallen in and out of love with each other a thousand times. If our hearts could speak, they'd confess that we've walked away from each other untold times. We've failed to honor each other with the names we've called each other to each other's face and behind each other's back; cursed each other for not recording checks; felt revulsion for each other's bodily sicknesses; and have gone off in our minds and married, bought homes, and had children with others fitter and finer than the one we're wedded to—all of this we have done zillions of times.

And we've returned to each other again and again, remarkably, mysteriously, wondrously, begging each other's forgiveness, sheepishly, desperately, earnestly, disremembering what it was that drove us away, pledging again to talk before giving in to the urge to walk away.

We keep coming back to each other. To keep a vow is not to keep from breaking it but to keep trying to discover its meaning. It takes only a few moments to make the vow but a lifetime to live it. I stagger to believe that it's me, the woman who at thirty-seven was too old to be given away. But she now gives herself away daily, repeatedly, to a man who she hopes will not be repulsed by the girl he finds her to actually be. In return, he gives himself away to her daily, repeatedly, happily, trusting that she won't in the end hate him for the disappointments he brings. I am a kept woman, and he is a kept man. We are kept by a vow too absurd to articulate.

> In token and pledge of my constant faith and our abiding love, with this ring I thee wed, in the name of the Creating, the Redeeming, and the Sustaining God.

If all that was required were a ring, we'd be home free, except that I laid my wedding ring down earlier this week and can't seem to find it. Where did I put that ring? In the same place I put the vow, I suppose.

We will marry and remarry each other every year for the rest of our lives. That is the nature of marriage, to marry and remarry this one person again and again, to renegotiate the marriage in light of the changes in each of us, to adjust in light of circumstances beyond our control, to marry each other all over again, if we must.

But talk is cheap, and we're both fickle. So we need vows. They won't keep us if we don't want to be kept. But if we want them to, they'll succeed in keeping us lying down and waking up next to each other, passing the salt to each other, picking up each other's laundry, picking up each other's clothes, and trimming each other's hair—until the love returns.

In the meantime we ride out the seasons in our on-again, off-again love affair with each other. Much like the on-again, off-again love affair both of us have with God. Now you see it, now you don't. In love today, not so in love tomorrow. Groping and searching for each other today, running away and hiding from each other tomorrow.

And because we're utterly incapable of keeping so preposterous and vast a vow, we need a marriage ceremony to make us accountable to the community. We need witnesses to remind us what we promised. We need God to teach us by God's own nature what really is love, fidelity, grace, and mercy.

Fidelity

Do this in remembrance of me.

LUKE 22:19

Odd, isn't it? The routines that make the least sense when we are adrift prove to be the very things that keep us anchored and facing in the right direction. I was never tempted to leave the ministry when I felt adrift, but there were many times I dreaded the duties and rituals that make up a large part of my ministry. I prayed over the sick, held babies up to be blessed, and arranged flowers on the altar—and stood outside myself, watching myself perform these tasks, which were by then almost second nature, scowling and shaking my head at times, wondering what in the world was the sense of doing any of this. Nevertheless, I never gave any thought to walking away. This is my life, I reminded myself frequently; I don't know any other way to live. It sounds like a coward's comment. And perhaps it was and is. Change unnerves me as much as the next person. If I had my way I would change only the things I want to change, and leave unchanged the things that suit me just fine. But labeling my failure to walk away from the church and ministry as fear is to miss the point. Attending church, preaching, officiating at the Communion table, and baptizing babies were precisely the things I had to do *until* belief returned.

The more I felt adrift, the more invitations poured in for me to speak in churches and the more I found myself having to act as chief celebrant at the Communion table because my husband was out of town and away from his pulpit—and I was the only other ordained minister. And while I whined and complained and threatened to stay put in my bed and pull the sheets up over my head until God sent me some sign, I always relented. I dragged myself out of bed, washed my face, brushed my teeth (but didn't always comb my hair), and showed up for duty. I needed to *do* what I was *doing*. I had to show God that I could be counted on to show up for my appointments.

Fidelity. Commitment. Trustworthy. Faithful. Devoted. For many years I didn't know what any of these words meant. As a

child of an alcoholic mother, raised in a home filled with domestic violence, having moved dozens of times by the time I
was twelve, abandoned, along with my sister and brothers, by
my mother when I was a teenager, I never knew what it meant
to be faithful to one's word, to stay, to be *here* and not *there.*
Imagine my absolute shock, the week of our worst, ugliest,
nastiest, take-no-prisoners yelling match, when my husband
returned home Friday night after work and after sorting the
mail rolled up his sleeves and began washing the dishes piled
high in the sink. Something inside me knelt. Fidelity.

I can't believe he plans to stay, I thought to myself as I held
back the tears, careful to keep my eyes glued to the evening
news. "Leave when it hurts" was the not-so-subtle message of
my childhood. Destroy it or leave it. Never did it dawn on me
that it was possible to live beyond the breach.

I once met a man who worked on the same job for twenty-
five years. Every Sunday morning for a quarter of a decade,
Jim Murphy has opened the chapel doors of a university
chapel. He has grooves in his right index finger from the key's
teeth marks to show for it. You have to know the grooves are
there in order to see them, just as you have to look for Jim
Murphy to know that he's there somewhere in the crevices
and bowels of the chapel building on Sunday mornings pid-
dling with the furnace, tinkering with the air conditioner,
banging on the pipes, fetching a lightbulb. When the dean of
the chapel introduced the older man to me as the sexton, Mr.
Murphy was standing in the front door with a bag of ice salt
under his arms. Mr. Murphy smiled shyly, tipped his hat like a
man born from another era, and like a mouse off to his secret
quarters, scurried away without a sound. "That man has
shown up faithfully to open this building, come sunshine,
snow, or rain, for more years than most of these students have

been alive," the dean said loud enough for me, Mr. Murphy, and the litter of college students standing around us to hear. "If no one else shows up, you can be sure Mr. Murphy will be here," the dean added.

Twenty-five years doing the same thing over and over again. Twenty-five years of doing one thing and that one thing darn well. Twenty-five years of showing up and being faithful to this one task. Opening the doors of the chapel for twenty-five years. Working as registrar for the university for twenty years. Typing correspondence and answering the phone at the blood bank for fifteen years. Teaching third-grade girls and boys for ten years. Serving Thanksgiving dinner to the homeless at the shelter for five years. Preaching to the same meager crowd of people Sunday after Sunday. Remaining married to the same person for almost all of your adult life. This sort of fidelity leaves me reeling.

I am ashamed to admit now that for years I have snickered whenever I attended the ceremony held at the beginning of each school year honoring faculty and staff people who have been employed for twenty-five or more years at the university where I teach. A tie pin, a bouquet of flowers, a mono-grammed rocker, a coffee mug, a crystal bowl, a set of pens—the gifts that institutions come up with to honor their loyal servants are the inspiration of the dull minded. But watching the smiles on the faces of the people receiving these gifts, I wouldn't know that they thought so. They actually seem pretty proud and content with their gifts. You'd think they'd received a medal of honor by the looks on their faces. I was mystified.

"Twenty-five years is a long time to do the same thing over and over," whispered a student of mine as we sat through one of these ceremonies.

"How unambitious!" I snorted.

But when Betty, a beloved secretary in my department, died from cancer the other year, and I realized that Betty, who had earned a twenty-five year gold pen from the university, knew more about my job than I did, I knew I had some re-thinking to do. Who knows better than a secretary the real workings of a corporation or university? Betty knew the prob-lems and woes of every student who came into her office, had secret knowledge of where things were kept and filed, knew the password for breaking into electronic files, held the key to figuring out which file cabinet held which folder, and had tucked away, in her blond head, who gets what and when. Twenty-five years was nearly impossible to replace.

In the highly competitive, ambitious, adventure-seeking, social-climbing urban professional world in which I have po-sitioned myself, it is rare to meet anyone who has stayed on any job for more than four years. Four years in one place and you've peaked, you're a has-been, you're in a rut. In a playing field dominated by appetite and impulse—where the luminar-ies move routinely so as to remain fresh, to stay on the cutting edge, and to get the salaries they want—staying put, blooming where you are planted, hunkering down, or how about just seeing a project through is an old-fashioned notion.

But the tedious, tiresome work of building an organization, or building a community, or building a marriage cannot rely upon orbiting luminaries. That work is done by those pre-pared to go the long haul, or at least to be reliable and com-mitted for as long as they are present.

People like Betty and Mr. Murphy belong to that rare breed from a bygone era who give their lives to doing one thing and that one thing well every day, faithfully, routinely, ritually, and if need be, year after year after year—not as mindless morons with no ambition or will to do or try something different, but as faithful human beings who are content to do what has to be done and then die.

"Didn't you ever get bored with what you were doing? Did you ever think of leaving?" a younger coworker once posed to a colleague. "Sure I did," he replied, "plenty of times. But there were also times when I wouldn't have wanted to be doing anything else in the world. You take the bad with the good."

Rituals, routine acts of fidelity, open us up to revelation because our devoted discharge of these seemingly empty, inane acts becomes an indication to others, to ourselves, and to the divine that no matter how ridiculous we may look, no matter how absurd the chances are of anything of consequence happening, regardless of what we feel or don't feel, we are serious about touching and being touched by . . . what? The other, angels, life, gods or goddesses, grace.

Yes, grace. That's what we have the potential of glimpsing in our daily rituals, that occasional, from-time-to-time, periodic, "now and then, here and there encounter with a New Creation," says theologian Paul Tillich. Rituals prove that we can be trusted to keep our appointment even when we aren't sure the other party will show up. They are done daily because the day is all there is. No one means to do anything for ten, twenty, twenty-five years. It was, at first, just a day at a time. Our daily rituals force us to act faithfully, dependably, honorably, with discipline, whether we feel these things or not. Whether it's opening the same chapel doors as a sexton for twenty-five years or typing the same forms as a secretary for twenty years, these acts show our persistence and readiness to weave a carpentry of entrance for the holy.

I awoke one morning to my husband's back as he sat on the

edge of the bed, hunched over, sliding his feet into one sock and then the other, followed by one shoe and then the other. He was deep in concentration as he performed this banal routine and didn't notice me staring at him in curiosity. I looked at him and wondered what I had gotten myself into. How could I love anyone who didn't have the sense to put on sock, then shoe, sock, and then shoe? For a moment, the man I married looked outrageous, stupid, utterly foreign to me. And I wondered whether I would ever be able to love him again for putting on his shoes and socks in this manner. The question was preposterous, I admit, and I was probably still dazed by sleep, which might explain why everything was distorted. But distorted as it may have been, it was as real to me as ten minutes later when he bent over to kiss me good-bye as he headed off to a meeting. I lifted up and puckered my lips to meet his even though I felt nothing resembling passion at the moment. I was disgusted with him. But I kissed him. I kissed him, despite my disgust, not only because it's our routine to kiss before departing. But I lifted up and puckered my lips on behalf of all the times that I've kissed him and not wanted the kiss to end.

Describing her routine as a writer, Flannery O'Connor once wrote that every morning she was careful to make her way to her desk whether she knew what she was going to write about or not. She stationed herself predictably at her desk in front of her typewriter faithfully every morning *in case* an idea came to her mind.

The inclination to walk away, give up, stop praying, stop believing, curse the winter, and withdraw cannot be denied. But I haven't, so far. I have chosen to dig my heels in and stick with my routine until the mystery returns. Bless the babies. Bury the dead. Pour the wine. Break the bread. Say the benediction. I have become grateful for these daily acts of fidelity, which serve to keep me anchored and disciplined.

One would think that as a minister I was already convinced of the power of rituals. But I wasn't. (Remember: I am the one who scoffed at the idea of doing the same job for twenty-five years.) I discovered, however, that rituals can sometimes do their best work when one no longer believes in them. It's all right not to remember why it's important to do what you're doing. I learned that every prayer needn't bring the intended results. Every day didn't have to yield mystery and awe. Every gathering with like-minded believers didn't have to end in an aura of breathless wonder. It was all right to celebrate the Eucharist and forget what the big deal was about celebrating the Eucharist. It's all right to pray over the sick even if the odds are that they will die before the evening dawns. There's something to be said about fidelity. I still can't imagine staying on the same job, or working on the same thing, for twenty-five years, but every time I consult a doctor with twenty-five years of experience in his profession and each time I board a plane where the pilot has fifteen years of flying under her belt, I admit to feeling warmly comforted.

Even after something in me had died to preaching, I continued to mount the pulpit and preach through the wintriest seasons of my soul. I climbed into the pulpit *just in case, if by chance,* so that *in the event that* some flicker of light, love, or belief in mystery returned, I would be there on holy ground to welcome and receive it back into my heart. And it did. From time to time, a lonely brush of air sweeps across the pulpit during a sermon, or while I am distributing the elements, or while I am singing a hymn. And it dawns on me again: "This is what I *do.*"

Chapter Four

The Mystery of Miracles

Eternal Life

For this is eternal life, that they should know Thee the one true God and Jesus Christ whom Thou hast sent.

The moment he began to speak, I knew it was God. But I didn't want to hear it. Stop. Don't. I can't listen. Why now?

"I didn't know any better," my father said, standing in my breakfast room. He stood looking out the window with his arms folded across his chest, a pose that once struck fear in me when I was a child. He was trying to talk to me about something, but I didn't want to hear it. His gaze was fixed on the trees in my backyard. I didn't trust myself to speak. "Do you take cream and sugar?" I asked, pouring the brewed coffee in a cup. You'd think a forty-something-year-old daughter would know how her father liked his coffee. But I didn't. There were a lot of things about my father I didn't know. And I liked it that way. But this morning he had something he wanted me to know.

"I didn't know I was supposed to go with you up to that fancy girls' college you attended. I just didn't know. I didn't know I was supposed to take a look around the place, check out the beds, inspect the cafeteria, meet your teachers, see where you would be staying for the next four years. You said you would be all right going by yourself. So I let you go by yourself. I didn't know any better." He shook his head. But he didn't look back at me.

"Two sugars, or one?"

"Two, please."

"How's Miss Marjorie's grandson? Did you say he's a student at Tuskegee Institute in Alabama? What's he studying?"

That's the way it is between me and my father. We can't talk about the past too long. More accurately, we can't talk about our past together too long. But the moment my father started fumbling for an apology about some past wrong between us, I knew God was speaking to me. He tried to apologize for something I never held against him, but failed to apologize for many other incidents we never talked about. But I didn't want to hear it. I didn't want apologies, but most of all I didn't want to have to forgive. That was not the topic I wanted God to talk to me about. Talk to me about flowers, children, the birds, music, death, or other people's wars. Don't talk to me about forgiveness.

So, exactly what have I had in mind all these months and years when I've complained about God being silent? What exactly did I want God to talk with me about? What was on my mind? American slavery? The Holocaust? Why newborns die? It's as though God pulled up a chair in my kitchen and said, "Why don't we begin with forgiveness?" No. No. No. Not forgiveness. Anything but forgiveness. Like the rich young ruler who walked away sad and dejected when he discovered that he had to sell all his possessions and distribute the money to the poor to achieve the eternal, I wanted all the benefits of the inner journey without any of the responsibilities that came along with that. I wanted God to speak to me, but I didn't want God to confront me.

Religious mystics for centuries have written of extraordinary experiences with God. Many mystics described their visions and encounters with God as frightening experiences. Even when God appeared in love, without any hint of confrontation or judgment, mystics have confessed to turning away, closing their eyes, or putting their hands over their ears. Even in revelation, mystics observe, God remains inscrutable. So awesome and overwhelming is God's essence even cherubim are compelled to cry, "Holy, holy, holy," and cover their extremities, observed the prophet Isaiah. When God appears, there's no guarantee you'll like what you see or hear.

I don't recall anyone from my parent's generation, when I was growing up, complaining about not hearing from God or not experiencing the presence of God. If any of them ever felt removed from God, as I do, no one ever talked about it. I don't think mine, however, is the first generation to agonize over its isolation from God. We're probably the first generation of both clergy and laity to lift our spiritual emptiness to an existential dilemma. We clamor for glimpses of God as though we were actually suitable to have dealings with God. My father's generation knew better. If God assaulted their otherwise mundane existence with occasional glimpses of mystery, they knew better than to expect such things forever. Their appetite for mystery wasn't as insatiable as that of my generation. It was enough for my parents' generation to worship God based on what they knew about God. Neither my father nor my mother is as contemplative and self-absorbed as I am—which means that both are spared the bouts of melancholy and self-loathing I sometimes suffer. With the inner journey comes great risks. Courting an inner life means running the risk of being changed. In our urge to know more about God we may wind up learning more about ourselves than about God.

I've all but given up on the idea of reencountering the God I met first as a teenager or the God I first started off with in ministry, when it seemed that all my prayers were met with God's brilliant yesses. I have managed to continue worshiping

God and, yes, even loving God, despite the fact that it has been years since I last felt God in spine-tingling ways. What I felt back then has been enough to keep me coming back to church Sunday after Sunday and kneeling by my daughter's bedside night after night all these years. That is faith, I suppose, learning how to live in the meantime, between the last time we heard from God and the next time we hear from God. And if during that time we have an insistent sense inside that we are being asked to forgive someone we never meant to forgive, to trust a stranger, to open our heart to someone or something we normally shut ourselves off from, to give up our right to punish those who have wounded us, then *that* is quite likely the beginning of our long-awaited encounter with God. When God does appear, if ever God does again, it will be to leave us not with intimate knowledge about God but with a painful, exquisite insight into what it means to be human before a loving God.

The Music of Noise

I
fall into noisy abstraction
cling to sound as if it were the last protection
against what I cannot name.

PAULA GUNN ALLEN

While I remain as convinced as most that there is no substitute for solitude and meditation, I am not convinced that noise is the enemy of contemplation. The task is to figure out which noises are worth one's attention and which noises can safely be ignored. It is impossible, after all, to live in a completely noiseless world.

At this moment, an old generator is pumping heat throughout my room and the musty sound inserts itself into my consciousness whenever I lift my head up from the computer, take my concentration off writing, and wonder what else may be lying around the room for me to munch on. There is also the steady hum of the hard drive on my Toshiba computer that tells me that it's safe to keep typing and that the computer hasn't crashed on me in the middle of writing this book. The noise from the generator I can shut out, but the noise from the computer I can't safely ignore. As a mother, a wife, a writer, a minister, and a professor I've had to learn that while it may not be possible to reclaim the silence I once enjoyed when I lived a solitary life as a graduate student in a dorm room, the challenge today is for me to learn to decide what noises are worth paying attention to. Some noises serve as helpful warnings of impending danger, such as the smoke alarm, signals at a railroad crossing, the ignition alarm that sounds when I attempt to leave the car without taking the key out of the ignition, the footsteps of a stranger in the dark behind me, the crash on a floor in the next room and the sound of my daughter's scream, the dreaded alarm in an airplane cabin signaling that the airplane I'm riding in is losing altitude. I never want to shut myself off from recognizing and responding to noises such as these. Noise can act as the voice of angels coming to impart to us important lessons on danger, love, mercy, prayer, and hope.

Changing planes in Charlotte, I am waiting in a comfortable, quiet lounge area for my next flight. I open up my computer journal to kill time between flights and to record a few random thoughts about dreams I've been having. The woman sitting in the club chair next to me speaks desperately into her cellular phone and begins to cry not so softly. She's asking someone about the surgery. It didn't go as well as hoped.

I keep typing this entry, pretending to be absorbed in my own thoughts although I am misspelling every word I type.

She's off the phone. She wipes her nose. She glances nervously over at me out of the corner of her eye. I don't look up. The air between us is filled with the noise of my typing.

Should I intrude upon her grief to ask about her pain, or not? She is crying uncontrollably now. Do I offer her my handkerchief? What is the difference between privacy and solitude? Everyone is beginning to stare—how can we not?—and here I am sitting the closest to her, pretending that I didn't see what I saw and overhear what I overheard.

Someone gets up from across the room and walks over to the woman next to me. Ah yes, my soul reclines. Perhaps the woman coming toward us will say something comforting and relieve me of having to. She hands the woman sitting next to me a pack of tissues and nods knowingly and warmly. But she doesn't say anything. She scurries out of the lounge. The only thing that comes to mind is the dumbest thing that comes to mind.

"Are you all right? I couldn't help overhearing you crying."

The crying woman doesn't say much, just that the news from her mother's surgery wasn't as good as she'd hoped. She thanks me for asking. There is silence between us—sort of, that is. The computer in my lap is idling. The screen saver has popped up and the hard drive is humming.

I would be hard pressed to say what just took place between us. I can't say that we connected or anything. Shortly after we speak, she gets up and walks to one of the bistro tables in the distance and continues to dab at her eyes. I sit feeling sort of clumsy. I finally got the nerve to say something and I feel dumber for speaking than for not speaking. Nothing miraculous has happened to reward my speaking up to this stranger. I wonder if I should have kept my attention on my typing, pretended I didn't hear what I heard, kept quiet. I don't feel anything. I'm still the same. I thought I would feel better for reaching out. What's the point? If I'm a better person for reaching out, I don't feel different. But I remember hearing a minister once say from the pulpit that some of the most lasting change takes place underground, like a seed planted in the fall, out of human sight, in the deep subterrain of the human psyche, in the dark, the quiet, slowly, deliberatingly, unnoticeably, mysteriously, during the coldest months of the year. That minister was me.

The woman continues to sit in the distance, dabbing at her eyes.

If it weren't for the steady hum of this laptop I might have died from the silence.

Lord, There's Been a Great Change in Me

People see God every day. They just don't recognize him.

PEARL BAILEY

I was glad I accepted the invitation to speak. I'd never been to western Pennsylvania. In fact, I try to avoid traveling to small isolated towns in out-of-the-way places. They make me nervous. I spend the whole time looking over my shoulder. This time it was a small Christian college in the upper Ohio Valley. I was the commencement speaker. More than three thousand people crowded into the large auditorium, and it was apparent from the moment their eyes caught me sitting on the dais that I was a rare sight in these parts. According to the school's Web site, which I decided to check out before heading off for the airport, the school's two thousand students hailed from nearby exotic places such as Beaver and Bucks counties, in Pennsylvania; Waterloo, Ohio; and Stubborn, New Jersey; and as far away as Keokuk, Iowa. The fact that they were Christians was supposed to alleviate any worries that I might have, but it didn't. It only made me more nervous. Anyone from a place that plasters on the billboard as you enter the town the words "Whoremongers and adulterers: God is going to judge you" is suspect in my eyes. Descendants of the eighteenth- and nineteenth-century revivalist movements that swept upstate New York, Pennsylvania, and parts of New England, most of the people from these parts are, I'm sure, good, decent, hardworking, devout Christian folks. But they also run the gamut of latter-day Pentecostals and charismatics. They are more oriented toward personal and inner transformation than to the intellectual refinement of their belief. As for their theological style, they take their Jesus straight and their Bible with no chaser. Our views on such things as family values, sexuality, homosexuality, women's roles, and Promise Keepers couldn't be further apart. But there was no way for them to know that, because I didn't talk about any of those things in my speech. I talked about God, and the power of love. To their credit, the people in the audience listened attentively and clapped enthusiastically when I finished speaking.

I spoke for less than twenty minutes and recall very little now of what exactly I talked about, except that it was something about growing up, growing older, growing spiritually, and learning to forgive things that previously seemed unpardonable; and before I knew it, the words were pouring out of me from a place I didn't recognize. I recognized the words, but I didn't recognize the place within. The words came out of me, but I'm still not certain that they came from me. Before I knew it, I was crying before three thousand strangers. Some of those present, who heard what I heard and felt what I felt, dabbed their eyes. A few in the audience came up and thanked me when it was all over. Many hugged me. Some kissed me. For a moment, I wouldn't have wanted to be anywhere else in the world. If I hadn't known better, I would have thought we had transcended our differences and felt something akin to love for one another.

The young female student, "born again," by her admission, who drove me to the airport was right out of some religious novel: perky, pretty, pious, chatty, naive, and dreaming of becoming a pastor's wife. (I didn't tell her I was married to a pastor, lest she ask me what it was like. She was too young to hear the truth.) She went on and on about the commencement and how she knew from the moment I opened my mouth that I was a devout believer. "It was apparent that God was speaking through you," she said, and asked what it felt like to be used by God. Thank God, she didn't pause long enough for an answer, because I had no words for her. She went on to talk dreamily about her pastor back home at the charismatic megachurch she attended in Philadelphia; her boyfriend, who was studying for the ministry; her recent experience speaking in tongues; and her love for the Lord. She wished out loud that her little college were, as she put it, "more on fire for the Lord" and asked me if I had any suggestion, since it was apparent that "you know the Lord in the pardoning of your sins." I laughed out loud, which she thought was odd, but I couldn't bring myself to tell her that it had been years since I'd talked with someone who took the Bible so seriously. But I assured her that if she prayed diligently, God was sure to hear and answer her prayers. Not the way you expect, I wanted to add, but didn't. She was too young, only nineteen. She had the right to an uncomplicated faith without me warning her of things to come.

By the way, she added, from meeting me she was glad to see that there are "saved" faculty members teaching at Vanderbilt University. I smiled and wondered how my own students back at Vanderbilt would respond to such a description of me. Of all the things that they might think to say about me, I doubted "saved" would be something one of them would think of. But I took her words as the compliment they were and tucked them away in my heart, where I store clumsy but well-meaning praise. Actually, it was I who was grateful—for having spent moments in the presence of a bubbly, Bible-believing sophomore. She brought back simple memories. She made me recall bits and pieces of a former self. The entire experience at the small, out-of-the-way conservative college in the Ohio Valley forced me to reexamine some of my own elitist attitudes about people who take what they read literally, especially the ones who believe that it's actually possible to love *everybody*. Somewhere over the years, I stopped believing the way they do; it was good to be reminded. For a moment there, I missed believing so simply.

Emmaus

I am interested in what prompts and makes possible this process of entering what one is estranged from.

TONI MORRISON

After all the powerful pronouncements of Easter Sunday morning, I was left with fifty days to kill. The banners had come down in the sanctuary, the altar was bare, the lilies were drooping. The organ was quiet. It was back to the silence. Until the next big religious feast, Pentecost, I was left to muddle along on my own. Arguing that I was too tired to preach and too consumed with getting done an article due in two weeks, I had convinced my husband that I was not the right one to bring the sunrise service message the past Easter morning. Every year I'd preached the sunrise service at his church. My preaching was almost about to become a tradition before I begged off this year. But I couldn't bring myself to do it this year. I didn't have anything new or fresh to say. After recounting the story of what I imagine as the women tiptoeing to the tomb at dawn, arriving first and without men, their astonishment at finding the hollow cave empty, and being the first to be commissioned by the Risen One to preach and proclaim the good news to the shivering disciples, I was fresh out of insights. I hadn't heard anything new to say, except that these days I felt more like the melancholy disciples than the exhilarated women. I hadn't seen a thing. I hadn't heard a thing. I had felt nothing. I hadn't encountered a soul.

Working for justice in the past year had worn my soul thin.

No one wants to fight for a cause that's losing ground. It had become embarrassing to talk about faith when one considered all the mad (and maddening) prophets storming the television denouncing working women, affirmative action, homosexuality, mothers on welfare. I couldn't bear to get into costume for Easter service and talk about the promises of the resurrection. I couldn't seem to get fired up about anything. Even worship was unremarkable. One would think that God would show for a celebration given in God's own honor.

But the most memorable appearances rarely take place in worship. They come when we least expect them. Community worship is helpful in making sure we rehearse the stories and the visions and reenact the myths behind our faith. But worship does not give us faith, and only on rare occasions is it capable of shoring up our faith. Faith comes, or doesn't come, in the struggle to live every day authentically and honestly.

The second-most-frequent question posed to me as a minister is, "How do I know when God is speaking to me?" or some variation thereof. Coming as it did on the week following Easter that year, I found myself at a loss for words. For the life of me, I can't recall what I said to the student sitting in my office the Thursday after Easter. She'd driven up from Atlanta to meet with me because she was struggling with whether to stay in school or to seize an opportunity that had just come up to teach at a secondary school in South Africa. She had the strange notion that I might be of some help in deciphering God's will. She'd heard me months before speak in Atlanta about the intimate memories the disciples must have shared with Jesus that allowed them finally to recognize him in his breaking bread before them. "Is it really possible to recognize God?" she asked—to recognize God so well that you can recognize his presence even though you can't make out his face? I don't know whether I was helpful to the student that day, though I'm inclined to think I wasn't. And if I've forgotten already what I said, then she probably forgot what I said as well. The answer I should have given didn't come until much later. As usual, it came to me the way most answers arrive at my door: *via negativa*.

Easter a year later, when I was off to Birmingham, England, to speak at the college of religion there, Queens College, I heard what I should have said to the woman in my office. Actually, the answer to her question wasn't to be found in England, or in the speech I'd carefully worked on for weeks to deliver to the religion students and the religion faculty there at Queens College. Rather, somewhere over the Atlantic Ocean, thousands of miles in the air, in the middle of the night as I tossed and turned in my narrow coach seat, seated next to a stranger, I recognize the bread broken right before my very eyes.

We know we are at the soul's portal, glimpsing mystery (one writer points out), when we begin to take notice of small things, both positive and negative. Take loose threads, for example. We begin to make out a faint thread of grace at work in our lives, patiently and imperceptibly joining the disparate patchwork of experiences that make up who we are. And while there is plenty that one can point to that argues against belief in grace, mystery, God, and the spiritual, still, one can't help but admit that there are moments in our lives, rare, random, and unforeseeable as they are, when we feel as though we have careened into the path chosen for us. These gracious seconds of grace break into our lives, leaving us more conscious of aspects of what it means to be created both human and a little lower than the angels.

Let me hold up one such moment for inspection, but I warn you it is a negative example.

For more than ten hours on the flight from Atlanta's Hartfield Airport to London's Gatwick Airport, I was wedged into a cramped seat in coach. On one side of me was the airplane window looking out over miles and miles of endless sky, and on the other side was a stranger who looked straight ahead for most of his waking moments and never said more than a few words to me. Fine with me, I thought. I didn't want to talk anyway. I had my books to occupy me. Armed with the latest books on God, justice, hope, and must-see places in London, I was happy to have ten hours to catch up on all the reading I'd not done in months. But that was before I discovered how difficult it is to read when someone you barely know is inhaling, exhaling, coughing, twisting, turning, and God knows what else within a few inches of your face. I could barely keep my mind on my reading for anger at myself. I kicked myself for not asking my London host to book me a first-class seat. This is what you get for not speaking up for yourself and asking for a first-class ticket for a ten-hour flight, I scolded myself.

When the man seated next to me shifted his bulk in my direction, leaving me less room than I had before, I was exhausted with self-derision. "Now this is what I call the missionary position," I murmured.

For more than ten hours, I was hostage to a stranger's body habits, and for ten hours he was hostage to mine, I admit. But the remarkably sad part about the entire trip, which is why it comes to mind now, is that for the whole ten hours each of us said very little to the other. For more than ten hours we took turns sleeping, snoring, tossing, turning, inhaling, and exhaling each other's air particles with hardly as much as a conversation between us passing our lips. He said nothing to me, the black woman sitting next to him. And I said nothing to him, the white man taking up the seat next to me. We directed our conversation more to the stewardess than to each other. Beyond the three times I said, "Excuse me," when I had to get up to stretch my legs and to go to the toilet, and the two times he felt himself leaning a bit too far over into my lap when he drifted off to sleep, we kept pretty much to ourselves for the whole ride between Atlanta and London.

Sad.

Two people sat next to each other for ten hours and never spoke beyond the civilized cordialities of "Excuse me." We acknowledged each other's presence only when we ran the risk of losing complete control of our bodily functions. We were—what?—too shy, self-absorbed, stubborn, filled with prejudice to venture out of ourselves to talk to each other. We shared germs but not words. We acknowledged each other's presence only when we were forced to do so—when our common, routine, ordinary need to take a leak or catch some sleep left us vulnerable. To talk to each other would have required that we see each other, listen to each other, put ourselves in the place of the other, and see the world through the other's eyes. And neither of us, for our own individual reasons, wanted to do that.

This is admittedly a negative example of mystery breaking into our domain. It surely isn't an example of one of my finest hours. But reflecting on it days later, after I'd arrived back home, I found that it succeeded in bringing back to me the question posed by the student a year before: how do I know when God is present?

The first thing I should have said was that we don't know, or rarely know, at the moment. We rarely recognize what we ought to recognize at the moment we ought to recognize it. This certainly applies to the people, encounters, and conversations that spring up to bless us. It usually takes us hours, days, weeks, months, perhaps years for most of us to realize, if ever, that we were visited by an angel. We're usually too preoccupied with our own thoughts, own prejudices, own self-interest to notice. To notice requires us to step outside ourselves and to put ourselves in someone else's place. Most of us are far too self-absorbed to do that. We would rather God strike us with lightning or make our car swerve around in the middle of the street for no apparent reason. Now, that's a communicating God, we think to ourselves. But for God to be in the shadows, inviting us to be vulnerable, to let down our guard, to relax, to trust the moment, is for God to be more than accessible. God has become demanding. "It is not enough to pay attention to what you are doing. You must pay attention to yourself doing what you are doing," wrote the Italian pacifist Lanza del Vasto.

Let me be the first to say that even now, almost a year later, I doubt that the stranger sitting next to me on the plane to London was Jesus in disguise. He was as rude as I was. And while I don't think that our nonencounter resulted in a colossal loss on either of our parts (neither of us was the other's soul mate, and we were both in coach, so neither of us probably had anything materially to give the other), we did miss an opportunity to be human. We missed the chance to broaden our worlds, to stretch our imaginations, to have our hearts filled. Engaging in conversation with a perfect stranger, inviting one into our space, and watching a stranger do something extraordinarily ordinary, like breaking open a loaf of bread and thereby opening our eyes, could have been precisely the kind of wonder both of us were crying out for at the moment.

For a moment, perhaps when the stranger was dangling in my lap or when I was about to lose it in my seat, the grace of God was lurking in the shadows. Perhaps. "See, now, put aside your prejudices, your inhibitions, your self-absorption. Be human." We could have perceived it—if only for a moment. But then it vanished, leaving us to the comfort of our prejudices, the real world, the is-ness of life. But for a moment there, only a moment, if we'd been paying attention to our bodies, we might have witnessed a resurrection of sorts.

The Last Day for Miracles

11 February 1995

I feel myself turning the corner. After nine months of chaotic silence, the desire to hear my thoughts out returned today. I woke up with an appetite for a well thought-out thought. I started a book this morning with the words "For everything I have learned there has been a season for getting it done." The season of my melancholy appears to be rapidly vanishing. The storm is passing over. Hallelujah!!

A miracle isn't a miracle because it defies explanation. A miracle is a miracle because it is experienced as a miracle. It happened at the time when I needed grace most, namely, on the last day for miracles.

> *The truly remarkable transformation is not the one from*
> *unbelief to belief*
> *nor from*
> *despair to hope.*

The truly remarkable (and frightening) transformation is from
dogma to wonder
from
belief to awe.

Today, awe returned.

Behold, I Show You a Mystery

You start out with one thing, end
up with another, and nothing's
like it used to be, not even the future.

RITA DOVE

On my desk near my computer is a photograph of a young black girl dressed in fifties clothes on her way to school that I cut out from the newspaper years ago. Her hair is typical of the way colored girls in the South wore their hair in 1957, a fresh upsweep of tight black shiny curls. What is atypical about her is the dark sunglasses she has on her face. One might wonder what would make a young girl put on such dark shades so early in the morning. The caption below the photograph explains everything: September 4, 1957, Little Rock, Arkansas.

The young black girl in the photograph is Elizabeth Eckford, and the photograph was taken of her on her way to Central High School. Elizabeth Eckford would be remembered in history as one of the first black students to integrate Central High. The photograph of her and the angry, jeering white faces in the background would become a symbol of race hatred in America. In fact, it's not Elizabeth Eckford's solemn stride along the streets of Little Rock that has captured my imagination all these years. Instead, it's the twisted expressions of hate and contempt on the faces of the whites looking on that has made me frame this photograph. The memory is worth preserving, I tell myself. How many times have I looked at the now infamous photo in American history and wondered what was going through the minds of the men and women on a beautiful September morning more than forty years ago? For years I held this and other snapshots like it from my own past against God. I couldn't understand what felt to me like God's silence. The sights and sounds of police dogs, firemen's hoses, marchers singing, protesters cursing, the Klan, lynchings, assassinations, four black girls lying in the blasted rubble of a Birmingham church. I felt like the prophet who cried out to God, "How long shall I cry out to you for help, and you will not listen? Or cry 'Violence' and you will not save? Why do you make me see wrongdoing and look at trouble?" Standing by and seeing the hard-earned political ground that blacks and minorities won during the fifties and sixties gradually eroded by the courts and knowing that those spearheading the move to reverse that legislation are from the religious right make it hard for me these days to talk with a straight face about a God who liberates. Whereas God's liberating victories in the Bible seemed always to be decisive, indisputable, and grand, those recorded in the history books since are less decisive, less spectacular, less indisputable, and are always having to be rewon. I could live with

God's silence in my personal life, I tell myself, if God didn't seem also to be silent in the public arena of human history.

Madeleine L'Engle penned a brave poem some years back with a first line that sends one reeling with its frankness: "I hate you, God. Love, Madeleine." The poem is a confession, along the order of Psalm 42 and other so-called imprecatory psalms in the Bible, in which the supplicant blasts God for some perceived failure in God's justice, morality, compassion. L'Engle, like prophets and poets before her, takes the time to detail the social crimes all around her that go unpunished and her protracted complaints to God that go unanswered. How many times as an African American and as a daughter of the South have I wanted to rail against God for some injustice I experienced or witnessed? I decided upon the Old Testament as my area of specialization because from as far back as my Sunday school days I have been obsessed with making sense of evil. From my first day in graduate school, when I set foot in my first biblical theology course with the eminent biblical theologian Bernhard Anderson, I was convinced that the answers to my questions about evil in the world and why good people suffer could be found in the Old Testament. I had great sympathy for the ancient Hebrew people and their determination to worship their God, Yahweh, despite the incontrovertible presence of evil. They seemed to be always going through a struggle, coming out of a struggle, or on their way to some new struggle.

L'Engle's poem is a favorite of mine because the poet doesn't conclude the poem with any safe, pat platitudes. God never bothers to answer the poet. Whatever healing she finds has come about through sheer confession. Sometimes when we're angry at God and galled at God's silence, the best we can manage to do is to confront God, confess our outrage, and risk speaking our minds. At the end of an unanswered prayer, L'Engle closes her list of outrage and disappointments with God with the conventional statement "Love, Madeleine." The journey from outrage at God to renewed affection toward God is long and bumpy. Praying honest prayers is the only example we have as our guide along the path.

Every time I look at the picture on my desk of Elizabeth Eckford I become sad. I can only imagine what words the tormentors hurled at the back of the pretty young woman as she walked, head up, back straight, outwardly calm but certainly inwardly terrified, eyes hidden by shades, through the crowd. Not only do sticks and stones break bones, but hateful words have the potential to disfigure a person deep within. For years I have wondered about the other faces in the photograph: Where are these angry white people now? Do these people still hate black people as they did back in 1957? Although I'm a minister, I admit that I've never held out much hope in their change over the years. I've been black longer than I've been a Christian.

Imagine my surprise in September 1997 when I received in the mail from people who knew my interest in this story a news clipping that had recently appeared in an Arkansas newspaper. It was the story of a woman who in 1957 had been an angry fifteen-year-old white teenage girl named Hazel Bryan. Now named Hazel Bryan Massery, and a mother and grandmother, she was in search of a way to ask forgiveness and set out looking for a woman whom forty years earlier she had tormented when they were girls of fifteen. Hazel Bryan was haunted by and hostage to a picture taken of her forty years earlier with her teeth bared and her face twisted with hate. After years of soul-searching and months of anguishing over where to begin, Hazel Bryan Massery found Elizabeth

Eckford. The new photograph is of the two of them standing together in an embrace on the steps of Central High School in September 1997, forty years after first encountering each other over a racial divide. Forty years later, both are different women, wounded by the memories but changed women nonetheless. Elizabeth Eckford, now fifty-five, is no longer terrified of white people's hatred, though no doubt permanently scarred by the memory of that September 4 morning. Hazel Bryan Massery, fifty-five, is no longer fascinated with hate, can no longer recall what she was afraid of, wants to offer history a picture of a changed self, though she doesn't and can't deny that the photo captured a girl she once was, long ago.

Is it really possible forty years later to rid oneself of demons from the past? Are any of us the same people we were forty years ago, hating the same people, loathing the same things, swayed by the same demons, afraid of change? "How do you reinvent yourself after years of conditioning?" I wonder aloud sometimes. How could we have been so wrong, so filled with hate, so overcome by evil to have said and done any of those things back then?

Of course, as a minister I take a certain delight in the sudden, grand, cataclysmic sorts of change that, as with Paul on the Damascus road, strike us blind and hurl us to the ground, and send us stumbling to the altar, crying, "How could I have been so wrong?" But real change, the kind we can trust, does not happen like that. "The change of life," wrote the English writer Katherine Butler Hathaway, "is the time when you meet yourself at a crossroads and you decide whether to be honest or not before you die." True change is far more gradual and imperceptible (at least at first) than we'd like to think, taking place deeply and quietly beneath the surface of the exterior self from which we speak, write, respond, and jeer. Before we know it, and without our knowing sometimes, we look around and we don't believe that anymore, don't hate that anymore. It's not a rational course, this road called change; rather, it comes as a result of a number of experiences that come together fortuitously at the right time, experiences that seem to suggest some kind of purposefulness working itself out in us, despite ourselves, and that when taken together seem to be pointing us in a new direction of thinking, living, and being it would be foolish not to follow. The blessing comes when those who are now changed, made aware of the probable harm done by a former self, are willing to return to the site of their past wrong and declare that they are wondrously, mysteriously changed.

God holds out for each of us the wonderful opportunity to change, change our minds, change the way we feel, change our course of action. To intervene, as the Hebrew prophets, as L'Engle, as I and others have demanded God do, would be perhaps to rob people of the opportunity to change for themselves. God could have caused some catastrophe back on September 4, 1957, to strike Hazel Bryan and the others standing with her, as I would have done had I been God. (Thank God I'm not God.) That would have shut everyone up. But it would not have changed their hearts. True, genuine change begins in the heart. It took Hazel Bryan Massery forty years to change. Many of us won't and don't have the luxury of forty years to wait. Every day something comes along that offers us the chance to change, begin anew, turn around, stop, and start over. A repugnant picture of an old self. The words of a child. The story of a victim. The words to a song. A chance encounter with a stranger. The voice of God.

A story comes to mind that I never tire telling my students, even though when they ask for the reference (as students are wont to do), I can't give it to them, because I've long since forgotten the book that bore me the story. Never mind. Just as well. Stories needn't be true to cheer the spirit; neither must they be told accurately to be restoring to the soul. Stories of faith *and* unfaith. It's in the remembering and telling of a story, Clarissa Pinkola Estes has pointed out again and again, that we find healing. Even inaccurate stories have the power to save us from despair.

Rabbis are assembled in a room, heatedly arguing among themselves, but more frequently with God, about the senseless suffering that Jews have had to experience throughout their sojourn over the centuries. They rail at God. They scold God. They challenge God. They shake their fists and demand God answer them. Finally, long past the hour for study and debate, when the clock on the wall announces that it is time for prayer, each man dons his prayer shawl and kneels in prayer, with tears of adoration and awe gradually making their way down each man's face.

I recall this story as a way of reminding my students that it is possible to lose faith and find faith in the span of a few minutes and in the span of a lifetime. True, life sometimes sends heartbreaking news of death and devastation and allows angry, ugly people like the old Hazel Bryan to come into our lives and challenge our faith in what is good. But it's also true that sometimes we look around at what is good, beautiful, and precious in the world and hear stories like that of Hazel Bryan Massery, of people changing and asking forgiveness, that make us kneel and cry and wonder why we almost let evil take that away from us.

In every class I teach, whether in the church or in the university, and every time my study in the Old Testament hurls me before the general public, invariably someone will come up to me to ask my opinion about some matter related to evil, suffering, and pain. What makes the questions of students and clergy, laypersons and agnostics similar in substance, if not always in content, and what usually sends these same people away eventually, dissatisfied with me, suspicious of my credentials, and still perplexed by this mystery, is the premise they all begin with: "If God is good, then . . ." We have Saint Augustine in his many explorations of the question of evil to thank for that formulation, not to mention the desperate desire within in the human heart to believe that ultimately, surely, for certain, of course—God, *pleez*—creation is in the hands of a just Deity. The premise keeps us going around in circles. For all the radical questions I've been trained to raise about well-meaning but otherwise baseless religious notions and have engaged in with relish in church and in the classroom, I must admit that here is where I am as stuck as the next guy. Put baldly: if God is not good, then why should I care that God is silent? God is probably doing me a favor and I don't even know it.

But I do care. I care even though I still don't have answers to the questions Deacon Foxworth, Augustine, and others as well as I have in good faith posed over the centuries about justice, suffering, evil, and faith. I care about life, about freedom, about hope, about beauty, about faith, about believing that somewhere out there, despite the overwhelming evidence to the contrary, a mysterious wellspring of energy exists inside each of us (or outside us) that creates, sustains, embraces, protects, comforts, and responds *also*. I care, even though a side of me suspects that the premise is the problem. It's all wrong. "Perhaps (swallow) . . . God (palms sweaty) . . . is not . . ." Nah! No time for that right now.

When the Bush Stops Burning

Where is the life we have lost in living?
Where is the wisdom we have lost in knowledge?
Where is the knowledge we have lost in information?

T. S. ELIOT

Evidently the gentleman from Texas has received my E-mail. I posted it to him three hours ago. Once again, I have unintentionally hurt an admirer's feelings.

> If you'd rather not be contacted, and if in fact, you turn resentful and condescending when someone tries to do so, perhaps you should notify those handling your mail server not to give out your E-mail address. Had I known that you were in fact cold and mean, that you didn't welcome conversation with strangers, I would never have written.

Judging from the last sentence of his message, which in a book about God is not appropriate to quote, he didn't bother staying hurt too long. He is now furious with me. In three hours adoration has turned to outrage.

Blame it on technology and the way it distorts reality. Equipped as we are as a society to transport images and to convey messages with nanosecond speed, the heart has little time to catch up with the cyclorama of information dashing across the screen. We don't know what to make of it all; but we don't know that we don't know. We think we know, just because it's *there*—right in front of your face, dummy. With the technological capability to dash off messages to one another in a flash comes the increased chance of being misunderstood and misinterpreted by those receiving information, and conversely the increased chance of misrepresenting oneself when sending a message. (In Internet etiquette, it's called "flaming.") In this case, based on one day sitting in the comfort of his living room and hearing me along with others talk on a nationally televised public broadcast about God, faith, and hope, the gentleman from Texas presumed some things about me. He presumed that I was—what? Well, accessible. But what does "accessible" mean in an age of virtual reality? The boundaries between fantasy and reality are blurred. Formalities are dispensed with: no introductions, no apologies, no request for permission to come in. Someone sees your face on television, reads your book, has a tape of your sermon, has access to your E-mail address, and he presumes he *knows* you. No need to do the hard work of creating a relationship, getting to know each other, working at it, learning each other's ways, learning each other's way of talking. Intimacy is here. Turn it on. What's wrong with you? Communication that should begin with "Hello" instead begins as it did with the gentleman from Texas, with "As I was saying . . ."

If we are equipped with the same information as those around the table and fully aware of the physics of fire and burning bushes, then what else is there to know? What is this knowledge that gets lost in information that T. S. Eliot warned us about?

Which brings me to ask whether I have presumed about God what the gentleman presumed about me. Have I missed something? Have I presumed to know God just because I have studied, read, and now teach all my life about God? Over and over in my Protestant scriptures I encounter stories upon stories of a communicating God, a God who is accessible, immanent, available, eager to be known. Moses' God speaks through burning bushes. The God of ex-slaves was disclosed by a pillar of cloud by day and a pillar of fire by night. Elijah's God comes in the still, small voice. Ezekiel's God fancies wheels. Job's God roars through the whirlwind. Through lost coins, lowly mangers, prodigal youth, sowers, seeds, and blinding light on backroads, God communicates, or so the story goes, to lost humanity. So, what's the problem? I thought God was accessible, knowable, communicable. I've told people that God speaks. How many times in the prayer before the homily have I and others echoed the judge Samuel and prayed, "Speak, Lord, for your servants hear"?

Now, after years of kicking against God's silence, I am tempted to conclude with the gentleman from Texas, "If you'd rather not talk, then perhaps you shouldn't have pretended to be open in the first place."

But what if God's silence is not a ruse? What if God's silence is precisely the way God speaks?

Then what was it that Moses witnessed in a burning bush out at Mount Horeb, if it wasn't God speaking? False advertisement? Misleading information? Someone relaxing in the comfort of his home, listening in on a conversation on public television with artists, scholars, and actors speaking passionately, intimately, movingly about God, might be misled into thinking that he has a right to jump right into the conversation—without any introductions, without knowing anyone around the table, without taking the time to build a relationship with anyone around the table, without proving that he can be trusted with what is shared. We speak the same language, American English; so, what's the problem?

Silence can also be an invitation, an invitation to communicate without words, without thunder, without burning bushes. In an age addicted to words, when memos, faxes, Post-its, E-mail, announcements, flash bulletins, cell phones, and news make talk cheap and easy, it is frustrating to be told that we must not rely on words—direct speech, that is. The burning bush was an invitation to be weaned off burning bushes, to come closer, to stay awhile, to learn idiosyncrasies, to commune.

God speaks through burning bushes to get our attention so as never to have to speak again *that way*. Perhaps it's when we confuse God's intervention with God's intention that we set ourselves up for years of fist-raising questions. For some wintry types, as Martin Marty calls them, there was never anything else other than silence. There's no memory of God having spoken so thunderously. A nudge was all there was. But whether there was a yank or a nudge, the fact remains that once you strike out in the direction of the pull, you'll rarely feel the pull that way again. The invitation is to take time to get to know the one yanking or pulling, enough so that it will be enough simply to be in each other's presence—enough to know that the other is in the other room, *or not*. Whatever. But wherever at the moment the other is, you are still loved, cared for, and will not be abandoned.

I have a friend who should own stock in Hallmark. She too is from Texas. She knows how to find and send just the right greeting card when I need it. I am amazed. I never seem to find *just* the right one. I find good ones to send, but rarely *the* precise one to send. Over the years she has become that "wintry friend" Marjorie Zoet Bankston talks about, who accompanies you through the isolation and loneliness, if you let her. She lives in greeting card stores, she tells me, whereas others, like me, live in bookstores. I rarely send her a card because mine never seem to equal hers. (Competition haunts me in kindness.) I end up calling and stuttering for something profound and encouraging to say. She probably has forgotten more than what she has remembered of what I've said over the twenty years we've known each other, whereas I will never forget her words. There's always enough power in them to make me stop and think. My favorite is about feeling comfortable enough in friendship to sit and luxuriate in the silence the two of you share, feeling safe enough to say things that don't have to be weighed, trusting the other to sift through those worth keeping and with a breath of kindness to blow away those that are not. Ah yes, I tell myself as I read her latest card. Listening for God is just like that. It's a kind of listening that requires you to stop, be patient, stay around awhile, suffer the quiet, and learn how to listen for God speaking to us through children, through ceremonies, through cycles, through caretaking, through Communion, through cards, and through the circumstances of our lives.

Bibliography

Elizabeth Bowen once wrote, "Certain books come to meet one, as do people." How true her words rang when the time came for me to write *Listening for God*. Many books rose up to greet and nourish me all the while that I muddled through my arduous journey, long before *Listening for God* began inserting itself into my consciousness. Some books that I read coincided with my writing. Some complemented my writing. Some changed my writing. So intellectually and spiritually nourishing were many of them I'm sure bits and pieces of their thought were carried away into my own thinking. If I had had to keep copious footnotes as I wrote this book, as is conventionally done when churning out academic publications, I wouldn't have been able to finish a page of writing. Readers too would have despaired because no one would be able to get through a page of reading for the insufferable footnotes. Still, I've tried throughout to point out when I have drawn directly from an author. But for those many, many occasions when the books others wrote not only met me but refused to leave me, I want to express my indebtedness.

Bell, Richard H., and Barbara L. Bittin, eds. *Seeds of the Spirit: Wisdom of the Twentieth Century*. Westminster, 1995.

Berryman, Richard. *Burning Bush and Broken Bread: Implications of a Communicating God*. Morehouse Barlow, 1987.

Buechner, Frederick. *Now and Then: A Memoir of a Vocation.* HarperCollins, 1983.

Campbell, Eileen. *Silence and Solitude: Inspirations for Meditation and Spiritual Growth.* HarperSanFrancisco, 1994.

Carse, James P. *The Silence of God: Meditations on Prayer.* HarperCollins, 1985.

Estes, Clarissa Pinkola. *The Faithful Gardener.* HarperCollins, 1995.

Heilbrun, Carolyn G. *Writing a Woman's Life.* Ballantine, 1988.

Heschel, Abraham. *Quest for God: Studies in Prayer and Symbolism.* Crossroad, 1990 (1954).

Holzer, Burghild Nina. *A Walk Between Heaven and Earth: A Personal Journal on Writing and the Creative Process.* Bell Tower, 1994.

L'Engle, Madeleine. *The Irrational Season.* HarperCollins, 1977.

Mairs, Nancy. *Ordinary Time: Cycles in Marriage, Faith, and Renewal.* Beacon, 1993.

Marty, Martin. *A Cry of Absence: Reflections for the Winter of the Heart.* Eerdmans, 1983.

Steindl-Rast, David, O.S.B. *The Music of Silence: Entering the Sacred Space of Monastic Experience.* HarperCollins, 1995.

Thompson, Marjorie J. *Soul Feast: An Invitation to the Christian Life.* Westminster, 1995.

Tickle, Phyllis A. *Re-Discovering the Sacred: Spirituality in America.* Crossroad, 1995.

Acknowledgments

Writing is one of those talents that don't get easier with practice. Every time I sit down to write I feel as though I have to poke around to find a new vein to slice in order to get the words to come. The most that a writer can hope for is to be surrounded by people who love her and care enough about her finished work to stand by with gauze and help bind her wounds when she has bled enough. I am grateful to have had just such people around me when the time came for me to sit down in front of my computer and poke around for the vein that held *Listening for God*.

I am grateful to my friend and agent, Denise Stinson of Stinson Literary Agency, who worked diligently behind the scenes bringing together the bits and pieces involved in publishing this book and in doing so freed me to write. My editor at Simon & Schuster, Dominick Anfuso, offered the kind of warm support and gentle editing that every writer needs. Special thanks to everyone at Simon & Schuster who helped make this book a reality, especially Ana DeBevoise for her patient requests and Victoria Meyer for her careful planning.

Finally, I am grateful to my husband, Martin L. Espinosa, who had to live for months on end with the wild mood swings and the mad ravings of a writer and never complained—except once, twice, or was it thrice? But who's counting? The man deserves an award. Special thanks to our daughter, Savannah Nia, who peeped into my study many evenings hoping to lure me out with a bag of hot buttered popcorn, not understanding why I wouldn't stop "bleeding" long enough to come out and see for myself the place where one can always find God, namely in the toothless grin of a six-year-old.

About the Author

Renita J. Weems is a writer, Bible scholar, minister, and author of *Just a Sister Away* and *I Asked for Intimacy*. She lives with her husband and daughter in Nashville, Tennessee, where she also teaches Old Testament studies at Vanderbilt University Divinity School.